I'm Never Alone

Ricky Shick

PAGE PUBLISHING, INC.
Conneaut Lake, PA

First originally published by Page Publishing 2021

ISBN 978-1-6624-3325-2 (pbk)
ISBN 978-1-6624-3326-9 (digital)

Printed in the United States of America

For my father, whose love reflected onto my life, and he shined every day of his.

CONTENTS

CHAPTER 1

Introduction to a Monster

It was early spring, and I had just celebrated my fifth birthday. My parents were renting a home for us in Naperville, Illinois, and I had to share a bedroom with my sister. But that was okay. The house suited our family.

One Saturday morning, I wanted to play outside. My mother told me to stay close so she was able to check on me from the kitchen window. She kept my younger sister inside with her. As I walked across our wet gravel driveway, I loved the sound of the gravel crunching under my new tennis shoes. I walked carefully, trying to keep my shoes clean. Evidently, it had rained the night before, and the outdoors were still wet. I walked and then skipped into our neighbor's front yard so I could swing on their new rope swing. To reach the swing, I hopped on a stone path that had been carefully placed on the grass. I had to jump back and forth on the zigzag-pattern stones, and this reminded me of playing hopscotch. It was so pretty where the flower gardens grew on both sides of the swing, and they scented the air with a mild, fresh, clean smell.

I decided to remove the warm sweater that Mother made me wear because the sun was heating the outdoors very fast now and the air was hot.

Under the swing was the typical worn, bare spot where everyone dragged their shoes to slow down or completely stop. I had to be careful not to step in the loose mud because my shoes might get wrecked. So far, so good, and then I always needed to jump up high to sit on the swing seat. I started pumping my legs to swing higher, and I noticed there were no neighbors outside in their yards. The normal outdoor noises suddenly become louder and louder by the second. My ears heard every sound near and far from me at an exaggerated volume. The airplane above me was so disturbingly loud that I felt like plugging my ears with my fingers. The birds flying overhead squawked very loudly, and I could even hear their wings flapping and hitting their bodies as they flew above. I knew this exaggeration of sounds was not normal for me. I wondered what was happening to me, and my heart started beating faster. I was very nervous as the perspiration started running down my face and pouring out of my body. I felt very anxious that something was about to happen to me, and it did! I looked back to our kitchen window to see my mother, but she was not there to protect me from whatever was soon about to hurt me. I instinctively turned my head to my left side and stared at our sidewalk. I felt very anxious; and I wished this situation was behind me, and I wanted the safety of my bed with the covers draped over my head. Horror hit me hard when I saw a girl-shaped form without feet or legs, which was floating above the sidewalk. I knew she was not human, and it was weird how she floated along the sidewalk path. I noticed she kept her head bent downward, and her hair covered her face. I also knew she had not seen me or heard the swing, which was still moving back and forth with me on it. I tried my best to be quiet and not make any sounds. I was amazed at myself that I actually saw her before she noticed me. Just a few seconds had passed by when I knew she heard the rope swing creaking as it swung backward for the last time. I had to drag my shoes through the mud underneath the swing to completely stop, but I never took my eyes off of her. I knew she was going to hurt me, but I wondered what she wanted from me. (Remember, I was only five years old, and I didn't know how to deal with this.) Now I knew she was a monster. She heard me and jerked her head up around to face me so fast it was as if she moved four times faster than a normal human. After witnessing this, I felt myself shaking all over, and I gripped the swing ropes as tightly as I could to steady myself. Before I knew it, she was floating toward me at a very fast pace. She moved over the zigzag stone path and never touched it. Now she was right in front of me and less than one foot away from my face. My breathing rapidly increased as I did not take my eyes off of this horrid monster. Now I saw what her dirty long black hair was covering on her face. She didn't have eyes, just big black holes that bore deep inside her head. Her mouth was the largest black hole in her face, and she didn't have lips around her mouth. Inside her mouth was just black and empty without any teeth to be seen at this time, but I didn't know what to expect later. Her skin was a white-gray color with black lines, which I decided were scars where she had been previously cut on her body. I didn't feel sorry because I hated her. I also noticed she had a slight movement from one side to her other as she hovered without legs. She smelled so awful I almost gagged, but I held it back. The odors from her reminded me of a dead deer carcass that was blown up from its bodily fluids, which had leaked out into the air I was breathing. This smell was mixed with the worst human body odor you could imagine and a sulfur smell such as when matches are lit. These odors combined almost made me throw up. Her smells of death surrounded me.

I was literally looking into her face and was horrified at what I saw. She was definitely too close to me. As I continued staring at her, she moved her arm and hand upon the rope I was holding so fast that it looked like a blur to me. All of a sudden, I felt a burning sensation with a lot of pain. She hurt me on the top of my left hand, just up past my knuckles. I wanted to scream, but I was too afraid. I realized she poked her sharp gray fingernail into the top of my hand. I continued gripping the rope as tightly as I could while she poked and pulled my skin toward herself and then dug deeper into my tissue. She gouged out a chunk. My blood immediately ran down my hand onto her finger as she removed her dirty fingernail. I also felt blood running down my arm and dripping off my elbow. From there, I assumed it hit the ground under the swing seat where I was still sitting. I never took my eyes off of her. I could feel the ice-cold air surrounding her as she stood in front of me, and at the same time, the sun's hot rays had heated the summer air. I felt sick to my stomach from the cold and hot air mixing and her odors blending with the pain she had inflicted upon me.

The monster moved her hand away from mine while I was still gripping the swing rope for security. I remained very still and quiet as I waited for her next move. Before I knew it, she was gone—vanished, disappeared, etc. She removed herself so fast that I didn't see her leave.

I looked everywhere around my surroundings, even above and below me. I had to make sure she was really gone. I jumped off the swing, and I missed the mud puddle underneath it. I realized I was shaking and a bit drained of my energy. I didn't want another attack from her. Mom was not at the kitchen window, but I knew I was in the clear from the monster; so I screamed bloody murder as loudly as I could for my mom. I ran to our house, and Mom met me at the door. She saw a lot of blood oozing out from the top of my hand and running down my fingers. I held my hand up high so she could see my entire wound. The bleeding wasn't as bad as the burning I felt inside my hand. My wound was cleaned, and I held ice on it to relieve the pain and also help with the swelling that had occurred.

I told my mother the story of the stinky girl who had hurt me on the swing, but I knew she didn't believe me. She never saw the monster, not even once. On that very same day, I cautiously walked to the swing accompanied by my mom for extra security. We looked for blood on the rope swing, and we found a lot. We also found blood on the ground in the mud. I looked for my chunk of tissue the monster had removed, but I couldn't find it. I thought that maybe a bird or a squirrel found it and ate it; maybe not! I still have a scar on my hand as a reminder of the attack sixty-three years ago.

In the story I have just told you, my monster is now sporadically haunting my sleep. I am sure this is happening because I brought memories and emotions back to the surface to tell you my story. I don't want it to enter my life again.

The End

CHAPTER 2

Come and Play with Us...Ricky!

I was still five years old, and my family and I still lived in the same house. This is when I saw the chocolate monsters in our basement. My little sister and I often played downstairs when the weather outdoors didn't cooperate. On one particular day, I was washing my doll's china tea set in the basement sink, while my sister was playing close to me. I noticed movement near the furnace on the cement floor. Slowly and cautiously, I walked step-by-step, closer to the furnace. I saw something brown oozing out of a crack that appeared to be about one-half inch wide but deep, which reached underneath the old octopus-styled furnace. As these slimy substances were moving toward us on the floor, they didn't leave slimy trails from where they had been before, and they didn't make any sounds. I knew they wanted me, and they also wanted my little sister. There was *no way* I would let that happen! I wasn't sure if just touching us was really their motive, but I soon realized they needed to crawl upon our skin and spread out their slimy mass. Was it to feed on us? I didn't know if they somehow wanted our energy or our sweat from playing a lot, or did they want our blood? The chocolate monsters needed to absorb something from us that they required for their survival.

Their appearance was as small as a medium pizza pan, and their color resembled melted milk chocolate, like a candy bar. They didn't have heads, legs, arms, or even eyes. I had never seen anything like these monsters during my entire life of five years. I noticed, as they traveled closer to us, they formed a bump for a head and two bumps sticking outward for arms. As they slimed very slowly across the floor, their bumps retracted inside of them. Gross. I believe they tried to appear more acceptable to me by adding human features, but they still did not resemble a human. To me, their gimmick did not work, and a monster is a monster.

They never joined their forms together with another. Only three monsters oozed out of the crack in the floor at the same time as they tried to get us.

Later, I told my mother all about them, and she promised she would be careful and wouldn't get hurt, especially when she washed clothes in the basement. If she believed me, how could she leave *us* alone in the basement to play when the chocolate monsters were down there? I knew Mother didn't believe me; she couldn't help it. She never even saw the monster in chapter 1.

As time went on, Mom kept sending my sister and me to the basement to play. I decided to go ahead with our playdays and make the best of it. I washed my tea set every playday, while I stood on a stool so I could reach the faucet. In the meantime, I had to constantly watch my sister so that the chocolate monsters wouldn't move too close and attack her. She always pushed a riding toy around the basement and furnace area. I knew what was going to happen, and it did. The closer she approached the crack in the floor, the faster the monsters oozed out from under the furnace. I always yelled to my sister as I nicely asked her to move away from the furnace. She always replied with the same word—"No"—because it was the only word she could pronounce. I knew all that, but it was annoying to me. She never listened to me, so I always ended up running and picking her up. I had to move her close to me, and I knew she never saw the chocolate monsters approaching us. They knew where she was at all times because they were hungry. If I had enough time, I would run back to her toy and retrieve it for her before the monsters could touch me. I made a game out of doing this.

I figured out fast that the monsters weren't very smart. They could have easily cornered us into a bad situation, but there was no strategy used by them.

Whenever Mom came down the staircase, the monsters retreated to the furnace and closer to the crack. It seemed like they were always sneaking looks at me. Mom never saw them, and she would always ask if I had fun in the basement. I always replied the same each time: "More fun today than yesterday."

The monsters weren't really scary to me; but they never changed their routine, and their mentality never improved. They were actually very boring to me.

Our weather improved considerably, and I was able to play outdoors with my friends. Very rarely did my sister and I play in our basement. The chocolate monsters still resided under the furnace, in the crack. They were never able to catch us!

Then my family moved to a different location in Naperville. I was happy to leave the boring chocolate monsters behind.

The End

CHAPTER 3

It Followed Me Home!

Now I was seven years old, and I knew I would never forget the horrid monster that I had previously dealt with in my life. We now had moved on to buying our own house in Naperville, and my entire family was very happy. I had met new friends at school, and we enjoyed walking around our neighborhood. This time together gave us a chance to catch up on new gossip about the boys in our class. I never told anyone about what I had seen and how I had been hurt by my monster. I knew they would say I was weird, and I actually knew I was.

Sometimes, my friends weren't able to join me for a walk, so I had to walk alone. My favorite place to visit was the cemetery. It was located on the far side of the train tracks, about three blocks away from our house. To reach it, I had to walk across an old rickety and wobbly bridge that seemed to fall apart, even more each time a car crossed over it. I had to hang on tight to the walkway railing because of all the shaking and swaying of the bridge from the left to the right. Below the bridge, there were sets of train tracks. I counted ten sets from one side to the other. I liked to stand on the bridge and watch the lights on the train's engine while it kept approaching closer and closer. The lights grew larger and brighter, even on a sunny day. I only walked to the cemetery during day hours because it was closed to the public in the evening. I wouldn't venture there at night, in the dark, because that would be spooky. (Haha!)

My parents found out that I visited the cemetery often on my walks. I volunteered this innocent information to them as I described how quiet, peaceful, and beautiful the entire cemetery was; and I loved viewing the gravestones. My mother and dad told me I was never to return there again. They also told me about train bums who took shelter under the bridge. After jumping off of trains that stopped at our town, they would take refuge under the bridge where they cooked food and slept there. Mother and Dad were correct because once in a while, I had seen a police car with its lights flashing, and the bums were being loaded into it. I knew what was happening, but I still ventured across the bridge. I thought I was safe if I ran fast and made it to the cemetery side of the bridge, and then I ran to a beautiful statue of Mary on the side road of the cemetery. All the roads in the cemetery were gravel.

I always walked throughout the graves, showing respect by not stepping on them. So many headstones had pictures of the deceased engraved on them. I always became teary-eyed when I saw an infant or child gravestone that sometimes had a detailed picture engraved on the front. Of course, I always figured out their age at death by the birth and death date, and that always made me shed tears for them.

Located in the cemetery, there were five religious statues placed among the graves. My favorite one was in the front section of the cemetery next to the paved street. It was the largest statue of Jesus that I had ever seen. He appeared to be burdened by carrying a large cross. He wore a long robe, which was tied in the front, and on his feet, he wore sandals. It was a beautiful statue, and it seemed as though he protected all who were buried there.

I had to obey my parents, so I later agreed not to cross the old bridge and walk throughout the graves. But I told myself I needed a "final and last cemetery visit," and this turned out to be a big mistake. As I had finished my last walk through the cemetery and saying my goodbyes, I approached the statue of Jesus, and for some reason, it did not appear to be normal. As I walked closer, I saw that both of his hands had been cut or broken off, and they were lying on the ground and smashed! The statue's eyes, which had been always comfortable to look at, had been punched and poked inward and had probably fallen inside of Jesus. They were gone! It looked horrid, and I felt terrible. I started crying and stared at the statue, then I said out loud with my sobbing voice how sorry I was that people had actually broken off pieces and defaced him. I noticed our daylight was turning into dusk, and I had to go home.

I was happy to see that Mom had supper ready to eat. I couldn't eat well because of the statue. I wanted to tell Mom and Dad about my final cemetery walk and how the poor statue was ruined, but I knew if I did, I would really be grounded for a long time. I did not say a word.

The rest of the evening at home flew by fast, and everything went well for me until we went to bed. My sister and I had our bedrooms upstairs. The staircase separated our rooms, and she always fell asleep before I did. She snored when she slept, and that was always my "clue" she was fine. I lay in bed and heard my dad lock the house door and then turn off all the lights. I remembered there were thirteen steps on our staircase. I had a habit of counting almost everything I saw or used in my life. I wondered why I was focusing on our stairs. I was still seven years old at this time, and I also focused on the statue and how sad I was to have deceived my parents about my final cemetery visit. I kept moving around in my bed, and I couldn't get comfortable. I started staring at the hallway at the top of the stairs. I felt anxious, and I felt something bad was about to happen to me. My heart started beating double time, and I broke out in a sweat all over my body. I kept myself very still as I lay in my bed, and I listened and listened and heard a noise approaching step by step up the staircase. It was now on step 9, which always creaked when stepped on. OMG, I knew it was the cemetery statue, and it was coming for me! It kept climbing each step as I counted, and I could hear the statue's robe swaying back and forth as it was dragging on the stairs.

By this time, I had to wipe the sweat out of my eyes so I could see clearly. My pajamas were also damp from all the perspiration, and my long hair was so wet that it became sticky and stuck to my neck. I knew it was the broken statue from the cemetery. I didn't know why a cement statue of Jesus wanted me. I used to like it, but not anymore!

Now it had reached the top steps. I knew my little sister was alone in her room, and I was worried it would get her instead of me. I could not let that happen, so I had to do whatever it would take to stop it. I shut my eyes and screamed and screamed for my mother. I kept screaming until I heard her running up the stairs, and then she was in my room with me. I told her to check my sister, and she was fast asleep and snoring.

I confessed to Mom about my day and all the wrong decisions I had made concerning the cemetery and my crossing the bridge. She assured me that I had just dreamed of a nightmare, but I knew I had not slept a wink. She said everything would be fine now, but I knew it was coming back for me tonight!

I lay back down in my bed, and I was so frightened—also still sweating. And now I was shaking again.

My sister seemed to sleep and snore through all the noise, which didn't wake her. She was fine. I concentrated and listened and listened, and then I heard it moving up the stairs with its swishing robe. It wanted to hurt me! It stepped on stair number 9, which made the crack sound again. I screamed and screamed, and this time, Dad came running up the steps to my room. I had hoped that Dad had scared it away. I had to tell him how I had disobeyed their orders about the cemetery. He then told me I was not grounded for my disobeying their rules. I was still shaking from being afraid of the statue. Dad told me being this afraid of the statue, as I felt, was worse than being grounded. He made me feel better, but the statue was still coming back for me.

Dad stayed upstairs in my room with me and sat on the foot end of my bed. He leaned his back against the wall. He told me to wake him in case he fell asleep. I felt so much better just knowing he was there with me and staying upstairs to protect me. I lay back on my bed and listened. I thought it might be gone for good. No, it was back again and climbing our stairs with the robe dragging on every step it took. At this moment, I immediately started to shake again. I had to move Dad's arm to wake him. I put my finger on my mouth and motioned him to listen. He carefully listened, and he heard all the sounds of the creaky step and the dragging robe across the stairs. He heard everything that I did. With the moonlight shining in through my bedroom window onto Dad, I saw his face turn pale white, and his eyes opened really wide. He quietly scooted off of my bed, and then he tiptoed to the stairs and stopped. He switched the hall light on and yelled and swore at the evil. He told it to go back to hell from where it came from. Dad saved me! I told him it wasn't really the statue but an evil spirit that we couldn't see. He said he believed I was right. Just like me, he never saw it, but he heard it and sensed it was there.

Dad sat back down on my bed and slept there until morning. I loved seeing the sunlight slowly enter through my window and into my room. I had not slept a wink that night, and it never ever came back to get me!

The End

CHAPTER 4

The Predator

While I attended my second grade in school, my friends and I joined Campfire Girls. My family's church graciously allowed us to use my Sunday schoolroom, which was located in the basement. Now I was able to go visit our church two times a week, and I loved it. I always felt safe and secure there. All of our Campfire mothers put together a carpool, which worked well with our rides from school, to church, and afterward, to our homes. Following one weekday meeting, all of the Campfire Girls had been invited to a birthday party. Our pickup ride to the party arrived on time at the church. I noticed when the car pulled up, it was very small and probably wouldn't hold all of us. My friends started piling inside and filled up all the front and back seats. Everyone except me was packed in tightly. We also had no extra room because everyone had to hold their schoolbooks, jackets, and birthday presents for the party. I asked the driver if my friends could put their belongings in the trunk to make room for me to fit. She told me the trunk was filled with groceries that she had just bought. Bummer. In the 1960s, people were not required to wear seat belts, and there was no limit on the capacity of people inside a car. So everyone except me managed to climb inside. I couldn't even get one of my feet inside the back-seat area. There was no room for me. The driver asked me if my mom was "possibly picking me up" and taking me to the party. I turned toward the car and looked at my friends, and I knew they were squished inside and anxious to leave for the party. My friends even gave me mean looks so they could leave soon. I told our driver that I wasn't sure if my mom was picking me up and driving me to the party. I knew I gave her that answer because I was embarrassed in front of my friends. That was my choice of words, and it became a big mistake for me. The driver said she would check on things for me at the party. My friends had overheard our "ride" conversation, and the driver was now relieved from worrying and satisfied about the "maybe ride" from my mom. This led the driver to drop all responsibility for me. I saw her worried expression on her face diminish as she smiled and quickly drove away, racing the car's engine with all my friends inside. They waved a sad goodbye, and I was left standing all alone. I felt that the driver couldn't get away from me fast enough. I don't know how that mother could leave me alone. I was only seven years old, and I knew she would not tell anyone about me being left behind at the church. I didn't know what to do next, and I wanted to cry; but I decided to suck up my tears.

As I glanced down the street about three blocks away, I could see the train tracks that I crossed over to and from school. I felt better seeing some familiar surroundings. I usually rode my bike in this area, and walking to my church would have been too far for me. At this point, I probably should have just started walking home, but I still wanted to go to the birthday party. I suppose I was still hoping a ride would pull up any minute and take me to the party. This was a bad decision on my part. I had decided to remain outside on the church sidewalk for a while and wait.

I looked down the street to my left side, and I saw the train tunnels' underground entrance located on the ground level. It was painted white; and only the top step was visible, and the rest were underground. I knew this tunnel well because I always rode my blue Schwinn bicycle along with my friends down the cement ramp on one end and through the long underground tunnel to the other side. I liked playing there because it was fun and a little dangerous at the same time. It was built many years ago for the train passengers boarding to or departing from their destinations. My friends and I never saw any passengers while we played there. It probably had a lot to do with the time of the day, immediately following our dismissal from school, and people were still at work.

Now I kept staring at the tunnel and remembering all the fun we had together. I remembered how wet the floor was with puddles of water everywhere, and the constant, cold moisture of being underground created a musty mildew smell. The old white-painted walls and ceiling had chipped white-paint pieces that gently fell through the air back and forth and down to the floor. My interpretation was that they looked just like large snowflakes falling from the sky. When a strong wind blew through the tunnel, it seemed as if we were in a snowstorm! I loved it! As we rode our bicycles through the puddles and then over the paint chips on the floor, they stuck to our wet tires. To me, this looked like a strobe light with the white chips stuck on our wet black tires and spinning in circles. The faster we pumped our bicycle pedals, the faster the black-and-white colors seemed to blend and then flash. That was a lot of fun.

Inside the tunnel, there were only ten small lights, spaced evenly along the wall and close to the ceiling. I knew this for a fact because I always counted everything; it's a habit. The light bulbs had small wire cages covering each light to protect them. When they had been mounted on the wall, they were stretched from one end of the tunnel to the other. They didn't provide the necessary lighting for the entire space, and most of the bulbs were broken or just burned out. I always thought it was dark, too spooky, and not the best place to be alone in the tunnel. The darkness was always inside, even on a sunny day.

As I still remained standing outside of my church, I became anxiously focused on seeing any person or even a car close by to help me. I heard the wind whistle as it grew stronger and louder around me. This gave me an eerie feeling.

This was the month of October; and the leaves were beautiful colors of orange, red, yellow, and brown. The wind tossed the leaves in a circular motion along the street and on the sidewalk on which I was standing on. It kept blowing harder and harder and then broke the brittle leaves into tiny pieces that blew into my face and became entangled in my long hair. This became very unpleasant for me. If only I could have only known at this time how insignificant this annoyance was compared to what was soon going to happen to me.

Located nearly on a busy street only one block away from my church, I heard a lot of traffic moving fast. Just like the leaves blowing in the wind, the cars also never stopped moving. Their engine sounds became louder and louder to me. I wanted to plug my ears, but I decided that there must be a reason for my hearing to become so sensitive! Next, my heart began to pound very fast in my chest. I could relate these circumstances happening now as it did when I met my first monster. I knew and felt that something horrible was about to happen to me. I stood as still as I possibly could while I stared at the entrance to the tunnel, and I could not take my eyes off of it! The tunnel was only three blocks away from my church.

There "he" was—the *Predator*! He was emerging slowly upward on the staircase from down inside the tunnel!

He took another step upward, and I could see his head with his thick, wavy black hair. Now with a couple more steps taken, I could see more details of his face with thick black sideburns, which reached down to his jawbone. The Predator's sideburns were even larger than Elvis Presley's. Every step he took brought him closer to me, and I was scared to death. I knew he intended to hurt me, rape me, and then kill me. I really didn't know what *rape* meant because I was only seven years old, and my mom and dad had never informed me on that subject. But I did know what the word *kill* meant. I knew that was the Predator's plan, and something inside of me was warning me.

I looked around my surrounding area, and there was no one anywhere to help me.

I also knew what was going to happen before he did. When he saw me standing on the sidewalk alone with no one nearby, he initiated his attack plan on me. He started by crossing the street to my side, and he began walking faster. He was now planning to end my life.

I sized him up within the little bit of time I had left to run. He was about one-half of a block away from me, and I couldn't move a muscle. He appeared shorter and smaller than my dad. I started crying for my dad, but I had to figure out my own plan without Dad's help. The Predator was wearing a long-sleeved yellow-and-black checkered shirt with washed-out, faded blue jeans that were falling apart. The jeans had a lot of holes, which had white cotton chunks spilling out with white fabric strings hanging down. His jeans were also covered with black soot, and so was his shirt. It sort of looked like some of the blacks were tar, and it smelled like tar in the air. He wore black ankle-high boots, which also had layers and layers of uncleaned soot. His oversized jawbone gave the appearance that he had been malformed since birth. I realized he had a learning disability by his body movements and appearance. I guessed his age to be thirty years old or a little more.

Now I knew somehow that he lived with someone who was his caretaker. He worked for the railroad and walked to and from work. He lived close to the area and actually lived just a couple of houses down from the church, probably close to where I was standing. This information really didn't help me at this time.

Now he was closing in on me, so I began walking to the church's side door. My walk turned into a skip, and I also sang the "Jesus Loves Me" song to comfort myself. He had actually slowed down his walking pace because he was checking his surrounding area to make sure no one was nearby to see him or to help me. He didn't want himself or me receiving attention from anyone. Now his attack plan became more aggressive. I entered the church and put my belongings on the floor near the door. I had been carrying my jacket, schoolbooks, and birthday present. I ran down the staircase to my meeting room, and I climbed into a coat locker. There were at least twenty lockers of the same size in a row. Once inside the locker, which was very familiar to me for using it at my meetings, I realized this wouldn't work because I couldn't lock the door. I knew I needed a better hiding place. I ran as fast as I could up the stairs, and I picked up my belongings, misleading the Predator to believe that I might have left the church. I glanced out the window next to the door, and he was just a few steps away from opening it. I kept watching him, and he was unable to see me. He was empty-handed and had to swing his arms way far out and back and forth to keep his balance. He was slowly approaching as not to draw any attention to himself. I clearly saw his face for just a few seconds, and his nose was long and covered most of his face. His eyes were small and beady-shaped and dark, probably a dark-brown color. I didn't really care what color his eyes were. I already hated him.

I then ran up the final set of stairs to the office and found all the lights were on, yet no one was there to help. I screamed for help, but no one answered me. I knew he would be walking inside any minute to find me. I saw three doors, and I tried to open each of them; but they were all locked. Now the Predator opened the outside church door. I froze right where I was standing, and I didn't breathe as he immediately ran down the stairs leading to the basement meeting room. I could hear him frantically opening and slamming shut the locker doors, which I had almost hidden inside of. He started yelling with his frustration, and then he growled in between his yelling. He sounded like a large mad dog. He was angry because he couldn't find me, and he wanted to carry out his evil plan for me.

I wasted no time, and I quietly crawled underneath one of the office desks to hide. He was now running up the staircase to the office as I quietly finished shoving my belongings way to the back so the chair and I fit underneath. I hurried and pulled the chair toward me and finished steadying the chair in place. Now there were no movements or breathing sounds from me. A horrible thought did cross my mind concerning the color of the clothes I was wearing. I knew my Campfire vest and beanie cap were a dark blue and blended with the darkness underneath the desk. I was more worried about my blond hair and my white blouse, which might catch his attention. I knew I had to accept this situation and pray to God for his help. Now the Predator was standing about ten feet away from my hiding place. There were seven more desks all lined up in a row with a walking space located next to the last one against the wall. I felt this was the safest one to hide under, and I don't know why.

Now I could see he was standing still and listened for me to blow my cover, but he continuously kept flexing his hands because he was so angry with me. I was glad I was small enough to fit underneath the desk, even with the chair pulled all the way inside. I knew my life was at stake. Next, he turned around and walked away from my desk. I continued watching him as he stopped, and then suddenly, he jumped up in midair and spun around as he yelled swear words and screamed as loud as he could. He landed on his feet facing my direction. He intended to scare me into moving my body or screaming with fear, but it didn't work. I knew he was going to try something like that. He made more uncontrollable growling sounds while he continued to flex his hands. He was so angry with me, and I hated him. Now he was punching his fist into his other hand. He just wanted to find me now. He walked closer to my desk, and I profusely started sweating. My sweat ran into my eyes and burned, but I didn't react to wipe it away. I also started shaking a lot, so I bit my finger really hard so I would stop shaking and not bump anything or make a noise under the desk. He stood quietly for a moment and listened for any kind of sound from me. He even held his breath to hear me and only me, but I held my breath too. His idea did not work.

Now I had a plan for him. I hated him so much. My plan was if he did catch me, I would fight back, scream, and mark him with my biting, scratching, and hitting him in the face. I decided to go for his eyes and poke my fingers into them to blind him. I would do the best I could to save my own life. My dad always told me, "Be strong, and then you have a chance. But to be weak, you have no chance at all." I missed my dad so much, and I wanted him to come and save me. I was constantly praying to God in my thoughts to please save me from the Predator!

Now as the Predator was standing too close to my desk, I could smell his body odor mixed with a strong smell of coal and tar. It made my stomach hurt, and I hoped it wouldn't make a growling sound. I knew he had hurt girls and boys before me and may have killed some of them. I was not his first and not yet his victim. He turned around with his back facing me and very quickly twisted his head, looking back in my direction. He was trying to trick me again. Now he faced the stairs and proceeded to walk down them to the outside church door. I heard the door open, and then it slowly closed by itself. No! I knew he did not go outside, and he had sneaked up the stairs to see if I had come out of hiding. There he was. The Predator was back, and he had never left. I had not even moved a muscle, and he was very disappointed that he didn't fool me. He yelled, growled, and stomped his boots on the floor. Then he swore at me and retreated down the stairs and out the side door. I quietly waited, and the door opened and then closed again, followed by dead silence! I did not move. I prayed for my mom to come and find me. All of a sudden, the door opened with a loud bang, and my mother's voice yelled, "Rick, where are you?" I screamed and cried, and I had become so weak that I needed her help to crawl out from underneath the desk. When I was finally able to stand up by myself, I quit crying, but I was still shaking. Mom hugged me tightly. Now I felt a lot better.

I asked her if she saw a man leave the church through the side door. I told her he was the bad, bad man, the Predator. She saw him walking from the side church door, and he put his head down so she could not see his face.

I told her he tried to catch me, rape me, and then kill me. We drove home, and I told her everything that had happened that day.

Mom told me she drove to the birthday-party house at the designated pickup time when the party ended, yet I had never made it there. She never received any phone calls concerning me waiting at the church from the other driver. Mom drove to the church, and you know the rest.

I didn't agree with what happened next.

The police were never contacted concerning the Predator.

The church was not notified of my encounter with the Predator.

My life changed that day, and I was thankful I was alive.

The End

CHAPTER 5

Blue Boy

Many years had passed by. I was eighteen years old and expecting my first child. It was time to find a two-bedroom apartment or a house to rent. We chose to move into an old farmhouse that had been converted into two separate apartments. I am sure the homestead's age was over one hundred years old or more. We rented the ground unit, and the upstairs unit was occupied by a single young woman who lived alone. She told us her schedule was very busy, and she was hardly ever home. She said not to worry and she would "catch up" with us later. We said our hellos and our temporary goodbyes until later, and we never saw her again.

Our son was born two months premature, but we were ready for his early arrival. Everything fell into place for our family, and we were very happy.

A few incidents occurred on the day our son arrived at his new home with his father and me. We walked inside our apartment, and we heard a woman's voice call out my name, Ricky. Immediately following, she said our son's name. My husband checked our entire apartment for the intruder, but I knew it was a ghost. I wasn't afraid, but it had taken us by surprise. There was no intruder to be found, and I did not like the ghost calling out my son's name. I didn't recognize the ghost's voice, but you never know if it was a family member who had passed and maybe not intending to scare us. I never wanted my son to be bothered by the paranormal as I was. My husband did track the ghost's voice to our only closet in the apartment. The closet didn't have a light, and it had two open doorways with no door. The previous tenant had hung long curtains from the ceiling to the floor where the doors should have been. Our handy flashlight was used to see when inside, but it was just as dark during a sunny day as at nighttime.

Late one evening, all three of us had fallen asleep, and a severe thunderstorm hit our town. We heard the loudest crack of thunder after lightning had struck a tree outside of our bedroom window. It was the month of July, and it was very hot even during the evenings. I felt as though I had levitated above my bed with all the noise. I ran and checked the baby, and he was smiling in his sleep. He was fine. It took my husband and me only a minute to realize the tree was on fire, and it was located close to our house. We heard the siren's warnings, and they were on their way to "help." I remained close to my son in the bedroom when I heard from an open window a familiar voice calling my name. I walked closer and asked who they were, but there was *no* answer. I recognized the voice. It was my girlfriend, Debbie. I called her phone at 3:20 a.m. and checked to see if she was actually home. She answered her phone, and she was not happy with me for the intrusion. I apologized and realized I had just fallen for a ghost trick of mimicking my friend's voice for the second time in my apartment. I'm sure the ghost heard Debbie's voice when she visited us, so it was able to mimic her whenever it wanted to. Wow, I didn't know ghosts could do that, and little did I know, there was a lot more they could do.

A few months had passed by, and winter arrived early with its snow covering everything outside. The time of the day was after midnight, and my son was sleeping; and I was sterilizing bottles, nipples, and also mixing baby formula. I was preparing for tomorrow's feedings. My husband worked nights, and this was my busy and after-midnight time to do whatever needed to be done.

I was still wearing my grocery-store pink dress from work because I had worked late this particular evening. Now as I stared out my kitchen window next to the hot stove, I noticed it was snowing outside. I also saw a small blue light approaching from a cornfield behind our house. I thought that was odd because there were no roads for vehicles to drive on through the field. The closer it approached, the brighter the light was, and it looked as though there was an object in the center. As it traveled toward me, it was only two houses away when I could see the light was radiating from a large human figure. Now the blue light was outside of my kitchen window. I opened my café curtains to get a better look, and of course, my curtains were blue. I saw that the figure in the center was a blue boy who was probably eighteen-or-more years old. He was a large boy who was wearing farmer's work clothes. He actually had many different shades of blue shining off of him, even from his skin. He appeared to be floating outside of the window and not doing a good job of it. He was a large, heavy, and strong-looking boy who kind of bounced up and down as he floated. He didn't hold himself stable in the air. I could clearly see he had dead eyes, which never moved, and there was no expression on his face. His long-sleeved flannel shirt had dark and light shades of blue, and he wore dark-blue denim overalls that were held up with blue suspenders. He continually stared through the window into my kitchen, and I didn't know what he wanted. I was frightened, and I did not want him inside our apartment with my son and me inside. My main concern was my son's safety. As I watched the blue boy, I grabbed the kitchen phone and called 911 for help. Three police cars pulled up into our driveway within a few moments. They had their lights flashing but no sirens probably because it was so late and at this time, normal people were sleeping. I did not feel normal with a ghost floating outside of the house and conducting itself as a Peeping Tom looking into the kitchen. A couple of officers entered through my front door, and four other policemen searched outside using their flashlights. They were looking for the blue boy and trying to find his footprints in the snow. I immediately led the police to the kitchen window where I left the blue boy for just a few seconds, and he had disappeared. I didn't believe he was gone! I checked the baby again, and he was sleeping with a smile on his face. The police had to witness my son sleeping in his bed because he was part of the police report.

I had to answer a lot of their questions about my 911 emergency call, so I did. They came to the conclusion that the blue-boy intruder had to have been seven to eight feet tall to have been able to look into my kitchen window. There were no footprints left in the fresh snow, and under the window, and I saw him levitating with his clear view of me from inside the kitchen. The police also checked the cornfield for prints and the yard at the house leading up to the window. They found nothing on the new-fallen snow. They also went to the upstairs apartment, but the tenant was not home. I talked with the police again, and I still insisted on what I had seen; so they tried to humor me. They told me I had probably seen a ghost that had worked as a farmer during his lifetime. Maybe this house had been his home, and maybe he died in the house. I knew I had seen a ghost. Not all of the police believed me, but a few did. They all left, and I was fine.

The remainder of the night was creepy, so I held my baby for the rest of the night as he slept, just in case the blue boy returned. My husband arrived home after work, and I told him the whole story.

On the following evening, the three of us had a date night together. We watched a scary television-movie marathon starring a lot of ghosts! We were also enjoying our stove-top popcorn, which I had cooked. All of a sudden, we heard the outside front door open and shut, then someone or something started turning our locked front door knob. My husband got up and unlocked and opened our front door, and no one was there. It spooked him quite a bit. A couple of nights later, it happened again. I called the landlord and told him of our experiences with the blue boy and the unseen person at our front door. The landlord proceeded to tell us the other tenant who lived upstairs had died a horrible death in a car accident two weeks prior. I tied this information together with our experiences at our front door, and I was sure the dead tenant was returning to our apartment house. The haunting continued with the tenant's lost soul just wanting to go to her home. I don't think she knew she was dead. The ghost became a visitor every two to three nights to go to her old apartment located upstairs above ours. Her haunting became more active as time passed by. I always heard her enter the house in the evenings, but my husband didn't hear anything because he slept a lot. Whenever she started climbing the stairs, I would count them, and I heard every step she took. I could also hear the old plastic liner on the steps make a cracking sound when she stepped on it. Her shoes also scraped across the wood steps where the plastic protectors were broken or missing. I never heard her enter inside her apartment, but that doesn't mean she didn't make it inside.

This was very sad and weird at the same time. We wanted to move, so we did; and we couldn't get out of the old farmhouse fast enough.

The old farm and house were demolished years ago for the completion of a town settlement. It represented pioneer days and life as it was back in time. I don't know if the blue boy or the woman tenant of the farmhouse still continued to haunt the area.

The End

CHAPTER 6

Are They Dead or Alive?

After we had left the farmhouse and moved into our own home, I realized my driving distance to my daughter's house was shorter than I thought.

She and I prepared a luscious meal on a Saturday afternoon for all her friends. The evening flew by fast, and I was the first person to leave near 11:30 p.m. I had driven my red Volkswagen Beetle, and the road I traveled on directed me close to a cemetery. I remembered witnessing one of my favorite paranormal sightings there. I drove farther down the road through a small, older housing district that contained only six homes. This small area was dimly lit with old streetlights glowing a dark-yellow light from each lamp's really dirty glass shade.

I continued driving, and I quickly had to slow down because I saw a few short people moving up ahead in a deep ditch along my right side of the road. I noticed the grass and weeds needed to be mowed, so I thought maybe everyone just looked short in that long grass. Next to the ditch was a cornfield that towered over everything else in the area.

As I drove on, I clearly saw three children running and playing in the ditch. They were each wearing Halloween costumes and carry-ing trick-or-treat bags. My car windows were all open, including the sunroof. I could hear their voices laughing, giggling, talking to one another, and just having fun. I knew it was *not* Halloween night, and the "young" needed a chaperone to guide them. The time was after midnight, and it was July, not October. I was a bit confused, but I wanted to find out why and what was happening. I slowly pulled up next to them while I drove on the shoulder of the road, and they were still having fun together. I yelled out to them from inside of my car, and I asked if they needed any help. No one even looked at me or said a word. Wow. I kept driving slowly, creeping along the road next to them, watching, and listening. The one little boy looked in my direction, but he never really looked at me. We had no eye contact with each other. There were also two girls who never looked my way. I guessed their ages were probably five or six years old.

One little girl was wearing a witch's hat and a homemade black dress, and the other girl was dressed as Dorothy in *The Wizard of Oz*. She wore a blue jumper dress with a white blouse underneath, and her braided dark hair looked so cute. She was carrying a stuffed toy dog wrapped in a blanket and tucked underneath her arm. I assumed it was Toto. In her other hand, she carried a white pillowcase for her trick-or-treat candy bag. The boy appeared to be the same age as the girls. He wore a sheet pulled over his head and body. His ghost sheet had a hole cut out for his entire head to be seen. His face was lightly painted white, and there was black paint around his eyes. He was spooky. The ghost boy carried a white pillowcase, and it had blue flowers embroidered on it. This embroidered detailing isn't used to my knowledge anymore, but I know it is an old, lost art.

The distance between the kids and me was very close. I could see their faces with their glowing, healthy, flesh-colored skin. I turned my car wheels a little to the right so my headlights would shine on them. I wanted to light their way through the long grass. To my surprise, I could see my car headlights shining through them and into the cornfield. I had a sneaky suspicion that all three children were ghosts. Then tears started running down my face, and I felt very sad for them. All three children were ghosts! I didn't believe the ghost boy was wearing a ghost costume. How many people have ever seen a real ghost boy wearing a Halloween ghost costume with his own real ghost head showing on top? (Maybe just me.) I felt very sad for him, but I knew all three children were residually trick-or-treating together and having fun. I kept following the children alongside the road and saw there was a *T* intersection coming up, and I needed to turn right or left very soon. I was careful to keep my eye on them so I wouldn't lose them. The ghost children turned right at the cornfield's end, and I did look away just for an instant to check for other cars nearby. The ghost children had disappeared. I turned right at the *T* in the road to follow the same direction they had turned. The ghost children were nowhere to be seen. I saw three white crosses in front of the cornfield. I stopped my car and got out and yelled and pleaded with them to please come back. I walked over to the crosses, and I bent down in the long grass in the ditch. Each cross had a picture of each child engraved in the resin crosses. It was a picture of their heads and faces on a circle on the cross. The date of death was on each picture, and it was the same for all three: Halloween, October 31, and then the word *Passed*. No other information was given. Now I knew these crosses were not their gravesites, but this was where their lives ended. This was so sad, and I cried again for them. I knew their hauntings together would continue and may never end. I also knew they had been hit by a vehicle while trick-or-treating, and all three were killed. This location was only a couple of blocks away from the town's cemetery. I'm sure their bodies were buried there.

I never had another chance to see the children again because we moved out of state, but I will never forget them.

The End

CHAPTER 7

The Crypt

My husband and I went on a short trip, which required a one-hour drive from our home to our daughter's house. We volunteered to help her move from an old house into a new home. It was located in a beautiful farm community in Illinois. We always enjoyed visiting our daughter and our grandson. Our drive directed us on country roads, which lead to another beautiful town. We had to stop at a large and busy six-lane intersection outside of town, which just happened to be located next to an old cemetery. Whenever we drive past cemeteries, I always look close and far back inside its perimeter for new graves, which are covered on top with flowers. I suppose that sounds morbid, but I can't help it because I always respect the dead, and I feel sad for the recent deaths and their surviving family and friends. I also look for family crypts or mausoleums. My husband and I sat inside of our truck during a long red light and waited for the stoplight to change. I was staring into the old cemetery when my ultimate wish entered my thoughts again. For over thirty years, I always have wished to see a crypt door slowly open, and I wished to see whatever it was walk out of it. I noticed near the front portion of the cemetery, there were three crypts. For some odd reason, I focused on one that had the largest front door. Some pillars were ornately placed, and it was constructed out of large cement sections. The outside walls displayed its old age with the black mold and green moss creeping upward on its walls and door. The family's name, inscribed above the door, was illegible because the exterior growth was covering it. Some of the letters were smoothed into the front wall from the weather's elements. It took many years to break down the letter inscriptions. This was an old crypt.

I kept staring and anxiously waiting for something to happen. I watched as the large cement door began slowly opening on the family crypt! OMG! Out creeped a black cloak-covered arm shape. The hood slowly moved outside, and then both arms pulled the rest of its body out. The creature's size filled the doorway opening. My wish finally had come true. The creature was finally out of the crypt. It was enormous! Its height was eight or nine feet tall! Its size had to have filled the entire crypt just by itself. I was so intrigued that a supernatural being had actually opened the crypt door and slowly crept out of it. As the creature slowly turned its back to me, I couldn't see inside its hood. Everything was dark and black. I didn't see any hands, fingers, feet, or shoes.

Now the creature moved and turned its back to me. It was now facing the inside of the crypt's open doorway. It moved one of its arms outward as if it were trying to aid someone who was stepping outside, and that was exactly what happened. Out stepped a beautiful young girl whom I guessed to be twelve or thirteen years old. Yes, the creature had helped her out of the crypt and onto the cemetery grass. The creature appeared to be quite gentle to the young girl. I looked at both of them and decided there was no way that the creature would fit into the crypt with or without the girl. He was enormous and tall.

At this moment, I had lost all track of time; and I told my husband, who was sitting next to me, to look at the creature and the girl in the cemetery. He still replied he saw nothing unusual. OMG! I did not move my eyes off of them. I knew if I did, they would vanish, just like the ghost children did in chapter 6.

The girl was dressed as a fairy princess. She had long, curly strawberry-blond hair and wore a silver-and-pink sequined headband. Her face was flawless with rosy-red cheeks a great healthy skin color, blue eyes, and red lips. I could see all these details because they were both in the cemetery and on the gravel road, which was close to our truck. It was also late morning—a sunny day and a blue sky up above. Her puffy fairy dress was dark and light pink with white chiffon that covered her entire outfit. She also had fairy wings attached to the back of her dress. She held a long silver magic wand with a silver star on top, which had long trails of pink ribbon flowing downward. Her legs were covered in white tights with perfectly pink-colored ballet toe shoes that matched her dress. I wasn't sure why I was also looking at a horrible, ugly, misshaped creature; and next to it was the beautiful fairy girl.

The creature put its cloak-covered hand on the crypt door and closed it very quickly with ease. As it shut, I heard a grinding, scraping cement sound, and I knew the creature was very strong. It appeared as though he used only his fingertips to slam the door shut even though I didn't see his fingers.

They both walked toward me, and it seemed that they never looked at me. I know they were aware of me watching their every move, so I just kept quiet and continued to observe them. Neither one of them seemed to care anything about me.

As they approached closer, I could hear a hollow sound crunching on the gravel as her toe ballet slippers crossed over onto the road. I heard a heaving, dragging sound as the creature walked with the girl toward our truck. I imagined it was dragging its tail as it was concealed under the cloak. I was in awe and excited about the creature's size and the girl's beauty.

As they approached even closer, it seemed surreal; and their clothing looked like Halloween costumes, which anyone could buy at a store, except for the creature's enormous size. The calendar month at this time was the end of August. They walked even closer to our truck as they followed the gravel road that surrounded the cemetery. I yelled for my husband to look again because the traffic light had changed, and he started moving forward with the traffic. I made my mistake of glancing at my husband and immediately looking back at the cemetery. They had both vanished from my sight. I was afraid that might happen. To this day, the old cemetery remains the same with the exception of new graves when needed. We have traveled past the same cemetery for many years since the creature-and-fairy-girl sighting. The fairy looked so alive, but the creature seemed to be "walking death."

My morbid wish came true, and it was delightful yet frightening.

The End

CHAPTER 8

A Black Mass

One weekend morning, my husband and I took a motorcycle ride near a town called Byron. We wanted to see a few acres of forest property that was for sale. During our ride, I enjoyed seeing two nuclear reactors near a river. Both were huge, beautiful, and frightening containing all of their power. Each reactor had enormous, billowing white clouds that were expelled from the top of each one and then blown upward many miles high.

We had previously scheduled an appointment with a realtor, and we waited at a designated restaurant. He never showed for the appointment, and we called and left messages; but he never responded. We left the area, and my husband drove on many back roads and finally found the property. Many years ago, when this incident happened to us, we did not have a GPS for navigating our vehicles. He parked our Harley in a cleared pull-off area next to the road. We saw the land and all the trees, which filled it. It was thick and, of course, a little darker inside from the sheltering, tall trees. We both enjoyed the warm, sunny day. As we stepped into the forest and removed our sunglasses, it lightened the forest just a little. We found a gravel trail and followed it as we looked around. Slowly, we walked deeper into the forest, and it became much darker and colder. I had to watch my feet as I took each step so I wouldn't fall. The gravel trail turned into medium-size rocks to walk upon, and it was not easy. We realized we were walking on a man-made, dry rock run-off. My husband assumed it was there for necessary drainage from surrounding hills and farm fields. While we continued walking and viewing the forest, I felt uneasy, and I kept trying to look beyond the tree trunks. I needed to see what was ahead of us. I was looking for something, but I didn't know what. It seemed to me the more time we stayed in the forest, the darker it became. I mentioned this to my husband, and he agreed. All of a sudden, the dim light inside the forest changed to a darker evening shade of dusk. We both looked up at the sky for a possible cloud coverage above us. The sky was clear and blue. I squinted my eyes and tried to focus on anything that had moved toward us.

There it was, a large black mass moving out from the corner of the forest. It was headed toward us. I had never seen anything like this before this day. I told my husband what I saw, and he didn't see anything. Now the mass had moved about an acre closer to us. I saw that it was huge, and it appeared to be as tall as eight feet and five feet wide. It had small, round-shaped, bright white lights that exploded, and then it seemed as though it regenerated more lights to explode again. The lights were as small as a piece of candy that never melted in your hand. The mass kept creeping closer; and I saw that it was translucent, and it kept constantly pulsating. It was alive and mobile, and it levitated about one foot above the ground. Whenever something was in its path, it moved right through it, such as when a cloud in the sky moved through the mountains. The air was ice-cold as it approached. I knew what it wanted from us; it needed our energy. It wanted to consume our bodies in its black mass and drain us, and I didn't know if we would die.

I grabbed my husband's hand, and we ran together as fast as we could, leaving the forest behind us. I couldn't run fast in my riding boots, so he practically pulled me most of the way back to the motorcycle. The sun was shining outside of the forest's tree line, and we had safely made it out of there. As I climbed onto the motorcycle, I looked back behind me, and I saw the black mass had stopped on the edge of the forest. It had to stay in the forest in the shade. It was pulsating very fast as it watched us scrambling to leave. I knew then that the sun was what could destroy it. I told my husband to gun it and get out of there fast. I kept watching until we drove down a hill, and I could no longer see the blackness. I didn't know what it was, but I did know it was evil.

Maybe the realtor had met the black mass!

The End

CHAPTER 9

Please Bless My House?

My husband and I decided to upgrade our home and move our family again, but this time, it was to a home that was only one-year-old. My son was ten, and my daughter was six years old. It took us almost three months to unpack and feel comfortable in our new surroundings.

One day, I decided to hang up a few pictures on our blank walls. I also hung up a wooden plaque that held long, tapered candlesticks. Two candles were joined together by one wick, and this was how I displayed them on the plaque. I thought this was unique. I showed the family the plaque and remarked to them not to touch the candles and certainly not to cut the wicks. Haha! I said that with humor, and we all laughed together.

The following morning arrived fast. I walked downstairs, and I noticed small footprints on my new dining-room carpet. This just happened to be the room where I had hung my candle plaque. My eyes immediately checked the plaque on the wall; and all the wicks had been cut, and the candles were no longer connected. I didn't believe that my kids would do that. I knew that my husband didn't do it, but I still had to ask him. He said no. I knew he had large footprints, not small. My children then walked into the dining room, and I showed them the small child-size footprints embedded in the new fluffy carpet. I asked for the truth, and they swore they did nothing. At this point, I actually measured each of their feet next to the carpet prints. Now I was shocked and realized there were no matches, and the carpet prints were too small. Whose prints were they? We all felt a little uneasy.

Early evening rushed upon us that day, and now it was bedtime. I always told my children good night and maybe a kiss if they let me. When I was in my daughter's bedroom, part of the nighttime ritual was to always close her two folding closet doors. On the following morning, I would always find both doors were pulled open. She was usually still asleep when I would notice them open. I believed her, but it was aggravating to me. This made me feel odd, but I decided to let this aggravation go and ignore it.

After our suppertime, we usually all retired to the family room, which was located on the ground floor. We liked to watch the news or sometimes, a movie. We began hearing something walking in my bedroom above us, and the sound seemed to travel into the hall-way. One weird thing to add to this was the entire living space upstairs was carpeted except for two bathrooms. We always heard heavy boots walking on hardwood floors. While hearing the intruder, I always imagined a tall man wearing all-black clothes. He had to have weighed over 250 pounds or more. It was loud. The distance between each footstep was enormous. When my children heard the entity walking above us, it scared them and also me. I always ran upstairs and checked every room, but I found nothing. We started turning the volume up louder on the TV to drain out the sounds. As time passed by, the heavy walking became more active at night and also began happening during the daytime.

It seemed to be targeting me more than anyone else. I was glad it wasn't picking on one of my children. Wherever I sat in the family room, the wall behind me had scratching sounds from inside of it and always behind my head. My family worked together by trying to ignore that it was directed to me. The scratching sounds were made by something larger than a mouse, and soon, pounding on the wall from the inside was also added for our entertainment. It was loud and sounded like a strong fist of a human.

One day, my neighbor asked me if our house had ever been blessed. I knew it hadn't been, so I thought, *Why not?* This was a positive action to be done, and I had high hopes that the noises and incidents would stop. I also wanted the minister to bless me once again. I had been baptized as a baby, and I was willing to try anything else positive.

Three houses in our neighborhood, including mine, had scheduled appointments with a nearby church minister. My house was the last one to be blessed that day. I saw our minister leave my neighbor's house and proceeded to walk my way. I was anxious and happy to receive help from our church. The minister approached the sidewalk that led to my front door. He abruptly stopped walking and stared at the front of my house. He looked upward and down and from left to the right in my yard, then he wrapped his arms around himself while holding his Bible. He appeared to be in deep thought. I continued watching and waiting for him to knock at my door. I could see him from a front window near the door. I was anticipating his arrival with my invitation to enter my home. All of a sudden, he took his phone out of his pocket and dialed a phone number. My house phone rang, and not to my surprise, it was the minister calling me. He was still standing outside of my house, and he told me he had to leave because of an urgent emergency. I never saw him answer any incoming calls. I put my phone down and proceeded outside to finish our conversation in person. I introduced myself, and he shook my hand and asked me if everything was okay inside my house concerning my family. I answered with "No, it is not okay" and that I had many questions that needed to be answered. He kept looking past me and checking the house. He asked me to reschedule another appointment date. I agreed, and I wished him a good day. I felt he was holding back information concerning my house. He never said goodbye, and he couldn't walk away fast enough to reach his car. The minister climbed inside his car and slowly drove past my house. I had remained standing outside, and I waved goodbye. He did not reply, but he was still fixated on staring at my house. This was a nonproductive day as far as the house blessing went, but the rest of the evening went well for all of us at home.

We had a positive incident happen for a change instead of a negative. We were all tired from the day, and all four of us wanted to watch a television show together. The wall scratching started, so we increased the volume. This was a normal routine. As I sat on the couch, I felt small bunches of my hair were being separated and lifted upward by someone's little fingers. Then they dropped my lock of hair and separated another bunch of hair and would do the same thing again. I knew what was happening, but I did not feel afraid. I sat still and didn't tell anyone that a sweet little ghost was playing with my hair. Then I smelled a wonderful scent of fresh linen. It smelled so clean and comforting that I never wanted it to leave, but the scent slowly drifted away. I felt this was a positive sign from someone who loved us. My daughter spoke and remarked on the wonderful scent in the air. I think this may have been the small child who had cut the wicks on my candles.

On the following day, I called the church for another blessing appointment. The secretary put me off by stating the church was busy and that they would call me to reschedule.

The church never contacted me.

The End

CHAPTER 10

Shadow Man

I was so disappointed that our house had *not* been blessed. All I kept thinking about was that I knew evil would soon cause me more problems.

One evening, I retired to bed, and I couldn't fall asleep or even keep my eyes shut. I kept hearing creaky and cracky sounds from the house, and I also knew which creepy sounds were the ghosts. The ghosts always wanted my attention and my acknowledgment of their presence. No problem. I always waved hello, and they were usually satisfied with that. On this particular evening, I realized why I was restless. There was something "different," and it was moving in our bedroom. Our room was really dark, but I saw a darker figure slowly creeping and sneaking along my far bedroom wall. I lay as still as I possibly could so I wouldn't scare it away. It moved closer and closer along the wall, either to exit the room through the open doorway or to move closer to me. I yelled, "Stop!" and to my surprise, the dark shadow immediately stopped. I'm sure shadow people do not take orders from humans, but I am sure I took him by surprise. That was my intention. Then I could see its shape with a head and partial arms' length down to its elbow area. It had a large trunk, but there were no legs. I knew this is what is called a shadow person. I wasted no more time, and I very loudly stated to it that I knew what it was. "So get the hell out of my house, and stay out in the name of our Father, who art in heaven." I could not stand the thought of human-shaped darkness creeping into our bedroom or wherever and whenever. I hoped I had scared it away, but I had my doubts. (My children were adults at this time and not always home, so the shadow man wasn't a threat to them.)

A few weeks later, after seeing the shadow sneak through my house day and night, little did I know it had changed its intentions and focused on me. One early evening, I needed to dry my hair, and the hair dryer was in my basement. I was relaxed with the warm air blowing my hair when I saw movement emerge from the other side of the basement. It was moving toward me. I immediately noticed this shadow was larger all over, and it was taller and appeared beefed up in a muscular appearance. It ferociously moved across the wall to attack me. It appeared as though it had been working out at the gym.

I was alarmed because I knew it was ticked off at me. Now he had returned to harm me. Maybe it was the same shadow man, or maybe it wasn't. At this instant, it didn't make a difference to me. I just wanted to be safe and far from it. I knew it thrived on fear, but I couldn't help being afraid. It moved closer and closer to me, and it grew taller by the second. I had an exit plan in my head, so I jumped up and practically ran right next to him as I vaulted the staircase up to the main floor of the house. It was following close behind me as I opened the door, exited the basement, and then slammed the door shut. I yelled and told it to go back to hell from where it came from. I slid on my back down the door to the floor and sat there to gather my thoughts.

I knew it could enter anywhere and anytime it wanted to. The shadow man did not pursue me that day.

I have seen more shadow people out of the corner of my eye, but I don't pay any attention to them. Hopefully they will continue to do the same.

The End

CHAPTER 11

Hellhound

A few days had passed by; and the time was after midnight, and we were all asleep. I woke up when I heard loud growling outside my open bedroom door. Within seconds, the growling had moved inside our room, and it sounded like a huge dog creature. It was invisible, and I followed its trail from the growling sound it made as it inched closer. It never took a breath. My husband woke from the continuous growling, and he witnessed this incident. I knew this was a hellhound. I sat up in bed, and we heard the hound's claws scratching the bedroom wall as it climbed upward. It ran on all four legs horizontally around all four of our bedroom walls. I followed the sounds it made of growling, snorting, belching, and its claws scraping as it encircled my entire bedroom. This was so scary, and I didn't know what it was going to do next. I also realized something else was really strange. As the hellhound ran across a large double set of windows that were covered with blinds, I never heard the blinds crushing from the weight of the hound. I also didn't hear any claws scraping the windows' glass. It made the sound of claws scraping on the drywall. This all happened so fast, and I was so scared that I couldn't move away from the unseen hound fast enough; so I found myself doing the crab walk backward on top of my waterbed as the hellhound kept running closer to us! Finally, it ran behind us on the wall above the waterbed headboard. It was still growling and making obnoxious noises, and it smelled of burnt hair. I saw the hound's lighter darkness as its shape walked slowly out of our room. It glanced back at us, and I saw its yellow eyes.

This haunting incident had ended for the night. My husband kept reassuring me that everything was over and we were fine. Yeah, right!

I crawled out of bed and turned on all the lights and realized I was shaking.

We examined all the walls and the windows; and there was no damage done, and nothing was out of place. I had expected the walls to be all scraped with hair and slobber and anything else a hound expels.

I never wanted to encounter another hellhound again!

Only two nights had passed by, and our usual disturbances continued to prey on my family. We were comfortably sleeping when a sound woke me. I looked to my left side to check the clock, and it was 3:20 a.m. I turned back over, and I looked toward the hallway. To my horrifying surprise, my hallway view was blocked by a huge hellhound's head. It was staring at me! OMG! I was shocked to actually see its head when our last occurrence was not visual and we just heard the sound it made. Now what was going to happen?

It was about five inches from my own face. It looked just like I had imagined it with a huge head, pointed ears that stood up straight, and its eyes dimly glowing yellow. I still heard the continuous growl that made me feel as though it was ready to pounce on me. I was afraid, but I didn't take my eyes off of it. The hound was also weird because it never blinked its eyes or even moved its head. I knew something was soon to happen, so I slowly pulled myself up to a sitting position on my bed. I cautiously pulled my right arm out from under the covers, and I formed a fist. I punched it square in the face, and I screamed as my fist went right through the hound's head as if it were a cloud of smoke. My scream woke my husband. He had no idea what had just happened.

I found that everything that had been on my nightstand was now on the floor. Everything had been hit by my fist as it went through the hellhound's head. I broke my lamp, which was trashed beyond repair, and I didn't care. I was glad to be safe and glad it was gone for now!

The End

CHAPTER 12

Fan People and "Red"

The following evening proved to be a night I will never forget. I was still really worn out and exhausted from the previous hellhound excitement. We went to bed around 10:00 p.m., and I placed a fan in our room because of the hot, stuffy heat upstairs. I was relaxed in bed with my head slowly sinking into my soft pillow when I suddenly heard a woman talking in our master bathroom shower. I listened, but I couldn't understand all of her words. The word *she* was said often, and the ghost was referring to me. This female ghost was talking to a male ghost, and he only replied with a yes or no. My husband did not hear their voices, but I did. I quietly left my bed and tiptoed into the bathroom. I jumped inside the small room; and I just saw darkness, and nothing was in the shower. I had to yell anyway because I wanted the element of surprise to scare them. It was dead quiet, and I continued to tell them I didn't appreciate them referring the word *she* to me. I also told them to get out of my house and please show some respect and let us sleep. It became dead quiet upstairs, and on my walk back to bed, I turned the fan up one notch faster. The fan motor was louder, and the blades spun faster. I was sure that the humming would help me sleep.

A noise woke me at 3:33 a.m., and I sat up in bed and heard old music from probably the big old bands such as Benny Goodman and all of its horns and orchestra playing music. I also heard a huge audience clap their hands after each song. I pictured in my mind that the women were wearing fringe, flapper dresses and feather headbands. This music dated itself back to the 1920s.

The music continued with men speaking very clearly about the next title of the following song. I pictured the men wearing their three-piece suits as they spun their dancing partners in circles in the nightclubs back in time.

I tried to stay awake, but I eventually fell asleep. I loved hearing the music. The following morning, I told my husband about the music I had heard, so we planned to try to hear it again together the next evening; and we did.

On our second night of listening to the entertainment from the past, we actually heard a commercial being repeated from the fan. They were the exact television commercials we had seen and heard that same evening. It was very odd. I could also hear music from my dishwasher when the fan was being used for heat and air-drying.

The following evening had a big surprise in store for me. I woke up from a loud crashing sound, and I sat up and looked around my bedroom. I saw the color red through my eyes. Our bedroom night light glowed with a light-red color, and our walls were dark red. My carpet and my bulldog, who was sleeping on the floor, were all different shades of red. I was very alarmed, so I left my bed and walked to the bathroom. On the way, I looked into my closet and switched on my light. All my clothes, shoes, hats, etc. were different shades of red. The bathroom was filled with bright lights, but everything was red with no exceptions. I looked at myself in the large bathroom mirror; and my skin, eyes, hair, and nightgown were red. I was a little upset, but I decided to try to sleep and deal with whatever the morning would bring. I felt fine, so I went to bed; and I woke with normal vision the next morning. This weird problem was gone for now.

I told my husband about my red vision, and he thought I had been dreaming. I also knew that evil had targeted the red vision to me because it was anxious to see me freak out. I did not react in a frightened manner, and I'm sure evil was disappointed at my reactions. (Haha!)

Almost two weeks later, my red vision reappeared during the daytime. It started quickly as though something just snapped its fingers and I was in a red-colored world again. I was actually washing dishes when everything turned red for a second time. I went along with it, and I didn't mention it to anyone. It finally left me for a second time, and it had vanished by the next morning. My eyes were clear again. This scare tactic might happen again, but I am ready for it. I have never heard of this happening to anyone else except to me.

Two years had passed by with no "color red" occurrences. I have to confess that the color red was always my favorite, but now I have changed my mind; and I love the color orange.

The End

CHAPTER 13

Picture-Perfect

Many years ago when my two children were still living at home, the hauntings inside our house presented a problem for their friends to spend the night. We actually had the same haunting problems when their friends dropped by during the day. If the experience was too frightening, I would always volunteer to drive them home. I felt bad for my kids, and I hopefully had become a protector for them.

One Friday night, we all retired to bed after a stressful, haunting week and a lack of sleep. This evening, I noticed it was extremely quiet, and I felt as though there were no sounds heard anywhere inside the house. It felt like the air was being sucked out and dead quiet. Something very odd was happening, but I didn't know what or where it was going to take place. I didn't know what to expect. I alerted my kids about how I felt, but that was all I could do.

The following morning, I was first to wake up, and I happily expected a nice day for all of us. As I walked out of my quiet bedroom and a couple of steps into the hallway, I glanced into my daughter's room. I first noticed both of her closet doors were pulled wide open. I saw her lying in her bed with our "wall" pictures piled on top of her. They were pictures that had been hanging on the walls in all of our rooms upstairs! Now they were piled on top of my daughter and the rest of her entire bed. Larger pictures with frames were on the bottom of each pile, and then the sizes were reduced to small on top. I screamed as I ran to her side of the bed. I felt sick to my stomach, and I yelled out her name as I reached her. There was no response from her. She didn't move. She was firmly tucked under the sheet and blankets. They had been tightly tucked perfectly and tightly under her chin. I kept yelling her name; but she couldn't talk, move, or even move her eyes to look at me. I shook her bed because she was zoning on something in the air above her that I could not see. It was controlling her! Finally, I broke the spell she was stuck in. My bed shaking worked. I grabbed pictures off her and pulled her up in bed as I screamed for my husband and son to help us. She started to cry as I held her, and I turned so I could view the entire room. I knew the evil was still present, and it was watching and listening to the commotion it had created using my own daughter. I then yelled, "Whatever just attacked my daughter is a coward. Pick on someone your own size. Pick on me!" (Swear, swear!) Her small body still had pictures piled on her legs, so I removed them; and then we left her bedroom. We noticed even more pictures had been removed from my own bedroom when I had been sleeping.

We all went downstairs to get away from the picture mess. We were all very upset and bewildered about everything. This paranormal involvement with my daughter really scared me and made me angry. We all sat at the kitchen table, and we listened to my daughter tell us what had happened. She told us something that she could not see, held her down on her bed, and it didn't let her move. She did not see the pictures as they were piled on top of her and the rest of the bed.

I told my kids that God was always with us and his love protected us. We all felt violated, and I also knew I had invited the evil to focus on me and not my children. Not knowing what I was soon to find out, a form of hell was on our earth, and I would become its prey.

After we had talked while sitting at our kitchen table, we decided it was time to call our church again to request our long-awaited house blessing. I left a recorded message to our preacher to please call back to reschedule. This was an urgent request. We never received a call from our church.

I always had the feeling that I was being watched from the ceilings in my house. A lot of happiness had been drained from my children's lives because of the paranormal at our house. They both started to go to their friends' houses instead of coming home. I understood all of it.

My son told me he had recurring dreams of wolves with glowing red eyes looking inside his bedroom from his rooftop windows. He told me he was always awake when he saw them, and I believed him. His visions continued until he left home to attend college. We had installed a large set of blinds on his double windows, but he could still see their glowing red eyes through the blind's narrow slots. He said nothing more about the wolves after he left our house.

Back to a short couple of weeks after the picture attack on my daughter, everyone was a bit more relieved; and my daughter, son, and I kept an open conversation about anything and everything that bothered them. The kids started talking about the positives in their lives, and it helped all of us. Our daughter healed quickly. She endured this paranormal picture incident and bounced back even braver than before.

The End

CHAPTER 14

Dead-On

Our family's stress had decreased since the picture attack, and I was just waiting to see what would happen next. I did not have to wait long.

On a weekend evening, I decided to take a very long, hot, soaking bath. Of course, with hot water and a closed bathroom door, the steam quickly covered the large mirror above the vanity. I stared into the mirror from the bathtub as I relaxed from the bubbles and the heat. Suddenly, I noticed a line was forming in the mirror. It was as if something had drawn a line with their finger as the steam was wiped away. The artist was not showing itself, and it remained invisible. I said out loud, "What the hell?" The steamed picture continued growing larger, and I realized it was a woman's profile and torso. She had shoulder-length curly hair and a round face. There was so much detail drawn on the face that it reminded me of someone very familiar to me. The defined and profiled nose, mouth, and cheekbones reminded me of my dad. I thought to myself that this female drawing looked familiar. It was a picture of me! This drawing was so precise that it reminded me of a photo taken by a camera. It was perfect and precise, and I was clothed in my favorite sweater. Good grief, how was this possible for this entity to draw me on a steamed mirror? There were no drips of water running down the mirror. A lot of things didn't make sense to me. How did this entity know about my favorite sweater?

Now the invisible artist had finished drawing, and there was no other movement on the steamed mirror. I was actually happy and in awe with the finished drawing. I said to whatever was still present and invisible, "Thank you. I am so pretty in your profile drawing of me. I love it." At this time, I was still in my now "lukewarm bathtub," and I did feel uneasy being naked and knowing an entity was with me. I hoped that this was a good and positive paranormal occurrence. Maybe this was someone I had known in my life who had passed away. This scared me, but at the same time, it made me happy. This drawing was dead-on!

The following week gave me another chance for a long, hot, soaking bath instead of a quick shower. I was hoping the artist would return and draw another picture of someone I knew. I followed my usual procedure of filling really hot water in my tub and adding bubble-bath powder. Next, I closed the bathroom door. By this time, steam had covered the mirror, and the entire room was filled with a steam cloud. I was very comfortable yet anxious and wondering if the artist would ever return. I again relaxed in the hot, heated water, and I fixated my eyes on the large mirror because there was really nothing else to look at in the bathroom.

Oh my gosh, the drawing had already started! I watched, and I realized this time, it was the full frontal view of me from my head down to my waist. It was drawn ever so carefully without any mistakes. Wow, I was really impressed, and I wished I had my camera. I never thought this would actually happen a second time.

My thoughts switched again to who was this artist? Was it a ghost or a spirit, or could it be evil? I knew whatever it was, it was dead. In this second drawing, my hair was perfect, and my face did *not* wear a smile as I had in my profile picture. This difference with the smile missing actually gave me a sick feeling throughout my entire body. Something was not right.

In this second frontal-view drawing, I was wearing the same sweater as I wore in the first drawing. Whatever or whoever this was, it knew me too well. I felt a little violated in my privacy. Maybe my privacy had changed, and it became an item of my past. I'm never alone. I wasn't frightened, so I replied to the dead being right next to me with a "Thank you, and a great job." I left the tub area and opened the door for a gasp of fresh, cool air. All of a sudden, the entire drawing collapsed into runny water drips racing down the mirror and creating small puddles on the vanity below. My picture was gone. It was amazing, and I will never forget the two drawings. I did not want any more drawings of myself or anyone else.

It took only a few nights later when the "dead steam artist" drew his third picture. This time, the steamed mirror revealed a man with a three-piece pin-striped suit and a large top hat on his head. This man resembled the actor Charlie Chaplin. His head was slightly turned to his left, and he was staring at something lower in front of him. He also resembled a comic book or a cartoon character. He had a detailed round, sneaky smile on his face, beady eyes, a mustache, and a pointed beard.

I didn't like the drawing by the dead artist, and I yelled for it to stop. The artist didn't stop, but it drew faster and faster. It drew a long rectangular table with four chunky legs supporting it. Next, it sketched a coffin on top. The lid to the coffin was open, and it extended the lid up high. There was a body clothed in a long button-down black dress with her hands folded together as if she was praying. Her eyes were closed, and it was obviously me. The dead artist drew me dead and inside the coffin. He even drew me in a black dress that I owned and kept in my closet. Yes, that is what it wanted. It wanted me dead. I started yelling at the evil dead artist, and I told it to go back to hell from where it came from. I stepped out of the tub and grabbed my bath towel, and instead of wrapping myself with it, I proceeded to wipe away the entire drawing until the mirror was dry and free of any steam. I kept yelling as I opened the bathroom door, and I forbade it to ever return to my house or even confront my family and myself again in the name of our Father, who art in heaven.

Time had passed since this happened. Once in a while, I saw very ugly and ghostly faces that seemed to attach themselves to steamed mirrors, windows, and water reflections. They all crowd together with their faces pressed tightly against the next one, and they look like puzzle pieces sometimes fitting together or overlapping on top of one another. Eerie as it seems, they all stared at me. I tried to ignore them, but sometimes, I tell them where they can go and what they can do there.

I'm never alone!

The End

CHAPTER 15

A Haunted Hotel

Have you ever stayed overnight in a real haunted hotel? I have, and it was an adventure I will never forget. The Stanley Hotel is located among the Rocky Mountains and nestled within a beautiful valley town called Estes Park.

My mother, sister, and I rendezvoused at the DIA airport in Colorado. We rented a vehicle and drove on Colorado's Route 34 headed westward and up and up into the Rocky Mountains, which led us to Estes Park. When I saw the town surrounded by beautiful, snow-peaked mountains, I knew I wanted to live there forever.

Across the town from us and located on a hill, our destination, the Stanley Hotel, was glowing white among the sand-colored boulders behind it. The Mummy Range mountains tower high in the sky and make a gorgeous landscape for the Stanley.

The main hotel had vivid red rooftops and dormers jutting outward on an immense amount of property. The hotel and other matching buildings have different purposes for serving the guests. So I planned on exploring and enjoying my options during my next visit.

Inside the main hotel, we ate at their restaurant, and we also picked up coffees from the snack shop.

We had checked into room 407, and we each received our key cards. Each card presented different views of the Stanley Hotel and even wildlife that grazed and rested on the property. I chose for us to stay on the fourth floor because it is the most haunted level and I wanted some excitement. Later on, the excitement was the best!

We, three women, decided to walk through the hotel. We found an adorable gift shop on the main floor near the front entrance. I bought a lot of souvenirs for my family, and I had fun shopping for everyone.

We walked outside through the double front doors to take in the views of the most beautiful mountains I have ever seen. When I saw the immense Rockies, my mouth fell open, and my face turned into a beaming smile. My mother looked at me, and she knew I had fallen in love with Estes Park and its mountains. I snapped a lot of pictures of the view, but it is impossible to capture the pure grandeur of what the Rockies have to offer. To exist at an altitude of eight thousand feet or more truly gave me a sense of clean air to breathe, and the mild scent of pine was refreshing and invigorating. I had a sentiment of well-being and relaxation.

During our first evening, we ate dinner inside the main hotel's restaurant, and then we retired to the hotel bar. This was when I convinced the bartenders into naming all rum and Coke drinks *Redrum*! I had so much fun with everyone that I felt I was in a famous horror movie having a nightcap with the actors; but in real life, it was my mom and sister accompanying me, and that was okay. As we sat and conversed and met exciting guests, I actually had fun with my EMF detector checking the guests. With their permission, I scanned the guests from head to toe using my electromagnetic field detector to determine if they were alive or dead! I held it close to them to check and see if I had any high spikes from the dead guests. Everyone really loved part of the scientific testing. (Haha!)

Afterward, we returned to room 407 and prepared to sleep.

We finally retired to our beds where I made my little sister sleep on the side of the bed closest to the closet because I knew there was a ghost inside of it. She said she didn't believe in ghosts, but that wasn't a problem because I knew better. I slept with my EMF detector lying on the mattress right next to my head. I had the alarm, and the red-light flasher turned up to "high" so I wouldn't sleep through an encounter from the paranormal. I lay in bed, and I turned on the large-screen television to watch a certain horror movie associated with the hotel that we were presently staying at. The movie associated with the hotel played continuously on a loop. I might have watched its entirety three times without catching any sleep. Other channels were an option, but who would want to switch the channel? Not me!

Only two hours had passed by when my EMF blasted its alarm, and our bedroom was filled with a red flashing light. There was a ghost in our room, and I was excited to converse with it. To answer my question, the ghost would flash the device only once for "yes" and flash twice for a "no" answer. It seemed as though I was communicating with a child who had passed away from a childhood disease. His family had lived and worked on the fourth floor. Even though this was somber, we had requested our room to be on the fourth floor because most of the activity was there and it was the most haunted floor in the hotel. Don't get me wrong. There are many other hauntings throughout the hotel, and we found most of them during our three-day visit.

After the ghost child left us, we slept a short hour, and I woke to hear my EMF alarm. I saw my mom sitting in a chair that was in front of an open window, which was a dormer, jutting out from the roof. (It was a cute area to sit in.) I called out to her, but she did not respond; and she continued to have a strange look on her face. I thought for a moment that she might have been possessed. She finally answered me after a few moments had dragged on, so I assumed she was all right. I looked at the clock, and the time was 3:15 a.m. Mom asked me if I heard the beautiful music from outside in the courtyard, to which I confirmed that I did. We did not see a person or a radio to be seen. Mom remarked how beautiful the piano music sounded as I heard Mom's words. I realized the music was traveling throughout the Stanley Hotel and down all the hallways in different directions. We knew that F. O. Stanley's wife was a talented pianist thanks to the history tour that was offered to the guests. Mom and I also knew that the piano was not in the music room, but it had been moved out of the hotel for restoration. Knowing this, I assumed that ghosts don't always need material props to make sounds. Her piano recitals gave enjoyment to everyone. We sat and continued listening to the beautiful music when suddenly, my EMF alarm gave me another warning. I heard children running, skipping, jumping, and laughing as they ran down the carpeted hallway outside of our room. I immediately jumped up, ran, and opened our door; and I took a step into the hallway. I didn't see anyone. I kept hearing the children playing around me as if I were standing among them. I yelled to them, "Please wait! I want to go play with you!" I was abruptly pulled backward by the collar of my tie-dye nightgown and then back into our room. Mom scolded me and said, "Get back in here. You are not going to play with dead children." She would not relax her grip, and I was heartbroken. I really wanted to join the children. Now I can see how cute Mom's statement was back then, but it was not at the time. If you are wondering about my sister, she managed to sleep through all the excitement. I know she always used her earplugs. The following morning arrived too soon for Mom and me, but we still wanted our coffee lattes from the hotel's café. I noticed the closet door was wide open. I quickly took a picture of my sister with the closet ghost orb right next to her head. I knew there was a ghost in the closet! (Haha!)

We went on a paranormal tour that day where I caught a lot of orbs on film, especially in the billiard room. We also saw a special room with an entertainment stage. This room was a graciously gifted restoration aid, in addition to adding a new stage. A famous horror author contributed his efforts.

Our excitement at the hotel was never-ending. I wanted to see the decorative outdoor lights that lit up the Stanley's rooftops. The lights automatically turned on at dusk. My mom and sister were not interested, so they walked to the café for coffee. I strolled outside by myself to watch the light show. Soon enough, the lights were shining. It was peaceful to watch dusk settle in and blanket the hotel with the surrounding town.

As I was taking in the view, I heard something running and scraping its claws on the main hotel's front sidewalk. It was approaching me fast. I looked to my left, and I saw a large black animal was running in my direction. I stood there to watch it, only to conclude it was a king-size black poodle. Remember that I was from the Chicago area, and I was not very "hands-on" educated when concerning wild animals native to the Colorado Rockies. To my surprise, I finally realized that it was a (huge) black bear! Oh my god! I urgently looked around for help as the bear approached me. I was the only person outside, so I also looked for a tree to climb; but they were all too small and short for my protection. I wanted to run, but the lawn in front of the hotel was flat, and my father taught me that bears can run as fast as thirty miles per hour. I knew that I couldn't run that fast. Next, the bear started snorting as he approached. I knew he was smelling and picking up my scent. It was too late to run inside of the café because its doors were about twelve feet away. Now the bear was slowing down, and he actually sat on his rear as he slid to a complete stop. There was only about eight feet separating the two of us.

I remember my dad had taught me to hold my arms above my head as high as I could and to stand unconditionally still and silent. In doing this strategy, I tried to show the bear that I was bigger and taller than I really was and the bear should leave me alone. This may have worked, but the wind blew my long fringed purse, which caught the bear's attention again. This was when I lost my wishful thinking, which didn't help me at all. The bear was staring directly at me. I had hoped that the people in the café would hear him when he growled, but no one came to my rescue. I stared back at the bear with a lot of hatred gathered in my eyes as I imagined him mauling me apart until I was dead.

Behind and to the side of the bear's head, I could look inside the café window, and I saw my mom talking to someone and not yet looking for me outside. It brought me comfort to see her one last time before dying. I looked back at the bear, and I saw his two-inch-long claws had sharp and pointed ends. I couldn't help but visualize the monstrous hooks ripping me apart. Looking at his eyes, I noticed that they were dark brown, and they were fixed on me and my every move- ment. He growled at me again, but now it sounded more like roar- ing thunder. His teeth were larger than I expected in his wide-open mouth. I was scared to death, and I realized I had involuntary tears rolling down my face, accompanied by my shaking body. I focused on the bear's eyes, and my fear amazingly turned into hatred, but this was different because my loathing for the bear calmed me down. I stopped shaking. Now I portrayed to the bear that I was not a coward. I changed my state of mind. My end was near, so I created a plan.

When he attacked me, I was going to poke out his eyes or at least injure his eyeballs with my thumbnails. Either way, I wanted to blind him for the rest of his life for taking away the rest of mine. With my strategy ready, I looked at the bear with malice and watched his eyes change to a grave stare. Remember, he was still sitting on his bottom, and this gave him an eye-level look into my eyes. I knew he was going to make his move on me. I had a plan to run toward him just as he was beginning to stand, so I could use the element of surprise to startle him. I needed these few precious seconds to work in my favor to save my life. I took a breath, and I ran straight toward him. The bear made a loud sound in his throat. Maybe he swallowed, and he was confused at the same time. Before running into him, I made a sharp left turn and continued to run until I reached the handle of the snack shop's French doors. I entered inside, and I slammed the door shut behind me. I looked back at the bear from the safety of the hotel, and I saw him standing on his two back legs, growling and showing me every single one of his teeth. I moved back and away from the glass doors just in case he would break through them to get me.

I tried to yell, "Help!" and "Mom!" but I was unable to make a sound with my voice.

By this time, a crowd of scared, screaming tourists had gathered around the doors. I was actually pushed aside by them so they could get a better look at the bear. I, among others, watched the huge bear easily lope over the ten-foot fence outside the snack-shop doors. These doors were located next to the parking lot.

A hotel gardener saw the bear outside, and he guessed the weight of the black bear was at least 800 pounds to 1,100 pounds. I was a bit more relaxed, so I yelled for my mom above all the crowd's noise. I found Mom, and when she saw me, she said I looked as "white as a ghost." (I have seen a few white ghosts in my life!) Looking back on this incident that occurred in 2008, I was afraid of bears. I do not hate them, and I respect them.

During our last day at the Stanley, we walked down the beautiful staircase and through the haunted hallways that led to room 217. This room is the most haunted guest room that the hotel had to offer. I knocked on door 217, but there was no answer. We, three women, stood in the hallway and talked among ourselves until we were interrupted by a kind woman. She asked if we needed help.

After explaining to her that we wondered if 217 was occupied, she introduced herself as the hotel manager, and then she unlocked door 217. She led us inside where we were allowed to take pictures, and she educated us about the history pertaining to room 217. She told us the true story of a woman who had worked in housekeeping at the Stanley. Decades ago, this woman named Mrs. Wilson had been a full-time worker at the hotel. She also resided there, full-time, on the fourth floor. One day while she was housekeeping in room 217, a fire started on the floor below, which was caused by an exploding gas lamp, and it spread upward to another floor. She was badly burned and required constant care until she recovered. Mr. and Mrs. Stanley cared for and paid all her bills. Since her death, she has been residing in room 217 to take care of any visitors that stay there. Mrs. Wilson is very cautious about who she allows to stay. If she doesn't want a certain hotel guest, she will repack their belongings back into their suitcases. Then she places the suitcases outside the door. Before leaving room 217, I told Mrs. Wilson that she does a great job of maintaining room 217 and asked if she would show herself so I could take a picture of her. She allowed me to, and I have a picture of Mrs. Wilson. She is the largest orb I have ever seen.

Our stay at the Stanley Hotel seemed to abruptly end. We did not want to leave the hotel or the town of Estes Park. The deer and elk of the Rockies are known for walking freely throughout the hotel's premises and freely through town.

I cannot wait until I visit Estes Park and the Stanley Hotel again.

I can personally give witness to one black bear who visited at the Stanley.

The End

CHAPTER 16

Demon

After my fun Colorado vacation with my mom and sister, the summer was at an end. Work had once again occupied most of my time. I considered myself lucky and blessed because I really did enjoy my day job. I have now retired from serving as a licensed day-care provider for children. On the eighth day of October 2008, to be exact, my life changed forever. I had a scheduled doctor's appointment, and as usual, all appointments were running late. Finally finished and on my way home, my thoughts were focused on what to prepare for supper. I noticed ahead of me that the state road was under construction, crowded with workers, and my lane of traffic halted to a full stop. The sun was shining, and the sky was blue, not a cloud in the sky.

Across from my driver's side of the car and about twenty-five feet away from me was a child-size person. It stood at a height of four feet or less. It was standing between two moving and dangerous lanes of traffic. As it stood with its back to me, I could see the wind blowing its hooded cloak from passing-by cars that were driving by too close to him. The spinning wind blew its cheap-looking cloak back and forth. The child stood there, yet no one else seemed to notice him except for myself. I was afraid for his safety.

He wore a black hooded cloak that totally covered the top and back of its head. His cloak seemed to resemble a child's Halloween costume, which could have been purchased from a local store. I couldn't see a face because it was still standing with its back toward me. I didn't see hands or fingers sticking out from the long sleeves. I didn't even see shoes or feet because the cloak covered everything underneath, and its length spilled down to the street's chewed-up pavement. As I still remained in my car, waiting for the traffic to clear, I stared at the child, and I could see the sun shine through sections of its cloak. I started feeling a little sick to my stomach. Something was wrong, and I thought about how odd it was that he was wearing a costume. But this was the month of October, and sometimes kids wore costumes before Halloween. I kept watching him, and I hoped he would not get hit by a car.

All of a sudden, the child jumped straight up into the air of eight feet or higher. It completely turned itself around in midair so fast that I didn't believe my own eyes. He moved faster than any human or animal ever could. Now I knew I was in big trouble with evil again. It chose me out of all the hundreds of people that day. I frantically locked my doors and closed the windows and the sunroof. I wanted to floor my little red VW in any direction possible to get away! I was stuck in the middle of cars on all four sides. I was boxed in and frantically praying to God for help.

Before I realized that the short evil, which was wearing black, had disappeared in the air, it reappeared standing and facing me from outside of my driver's door window. Only the window separated me and the demon from hell. It stood facing me with its head bent downward, and I could see just a little inside its hood. I wanted to see what it was hiding!

The faceless demon didn't have eyes, a nose, or a mouth. The space under the hood was blacker than black darkness and contained small twinkling explosions that were never-ending.

I know why they bend their heads downward; it's because we humans would not be able to handle a faceless figure of evil.

The darkness inside the hood was also filled with other differently shaped objects, which were floating and moving slowly with no direction or guidance. The small explosions were very small and about one-fourth the size of a dime. The explosions were identical to what I previously saw inside of the moving black mass in chapter 8.

Another description, in my opinion, of the inside of a demon's hood was a sight we have all seen on television at one time or another. It resembled a view of outer space with exploding shooting stars spinning very fast. There is also a similarity to space debris inside the hood, and this was slowly floating. This debris bumps into other debris and also hits the inside the hood. I looked inside the hood very carefully to see what I had to deal with. I had no ideas, and I was afraid for my life. Why me? Did it single me out of all the other people because I could see it?

One split second later, the demon disappeared from outside of my window. I knew where it was! It was inside my car and sitting behind me in the back seat. I heard myself gasping for air. I felt its presence, but I couldn't see it. It made itself invisible, and this was horrifying to me. I turned around in the car seat and looked everywhere and felt everything with my right hand. I felt nothing but cold air; it was still with me. My heart was pounding fast, and I was gasping for breaths of air.

Believe it or not, the traffic started to move, and I had no choice but to do my best to drive without losing control of my car. I grabbed my cell phone and tried to reach my husband for help, but the line was just static. I became so afraid at this point that I felt an emotion overcome me that all this was not realistically happening. I thought I might be slipping into shock, or was it the demon making me feel this emotion? I fought this emotion and gathered my thoughts, and I focused on finding help for myself. I was okay. I just kept talking and praying to God for help.

I dialed 911 for emergency help, but the phone had no dial tone and just static. I just wanted a human to help me. While my situation was in "a bad way" for me, I kept checking inside of the car for the demon. It was invisible and quiet. I knew it was still with me. I realized tears were running down my face, and I was still shaking. My breathing had improved; that was good.

I noticed the sky was full of dark clouds and the cloud coverage was thick. I kept driving and soon would arrive in my town of Yorkville. I decided not to drive to my home because I was afraid for my husband and my dog's involvement. I didn't want the demon in my house, so I drove to church for help. The wind blew with strong gusts. The sky was almost black as I parked my car in the gravel parking lot located across the street from my church. There weren't any cars in the parking lot or any cars anywhere to be seen. Now the wind picked up the dust and blew it into my eyes and my body. Bolts of lightning were cracking close by me, and the thunder followed with crashes drowning out any other sounds. I had trouble shutting my car door because of the forceful wind. (I felt as though I was in Damien's *The Omen* movie!)

I saw a faint glow of light shining through a few stained-glass windows in the church. I really hoped the preacher was inside and I could get help. I heard a ferocious crack of thunder in the sky right above me, and it had a growling sound added to it. The wind slammed my car door shut, and I knew the demon was still with me. It did not like my church with the possibility of help waiting inside. I walked slowly against the wind and made it to the church's entrance. I pushed on the doorknob, and it was locked; and the other front door was also locked. It started to rain, and I noticed the office lights were on in the basement. I ran only a few feet away and down the stairs to the office door. I rang the doorbell, and a man peered out through the window. He yelled that the church was closed and the service was tomorrow morning. I yelled back and asked him to open the door because I needed his help. (This was not our preacher.) He gave me a hand motion across his neck and said, "Sorry." I was devastated and afraid to death. I screamed, "Help me, please!" The man shut the lights off, and I thought he decided to help me. The office worker somehow left the church out through another door. I was left standing with an invisible demon. I realized I had nowhere to go except to my home. As I drove through town, I kept repeating the Lord's Prayer and yelled it as loudly as I could. This gave me some comfort, and I knew the demon was still with me. I arrived home and exited my car as fast as I could. I made it inside my house and screamed for my husband. I frantically told him everything that had happened. I knew he didn't believe me. The entire day brought forth a supernatural evil into my home with its own plan to kill me.

The demon remained invisible and quiet, and it listened and watched everything we said and did. This demon could have manifested itself whenever it wanted to, but it was a coward. "It" wanted my husband to think I was slipping into insanity.

We made it frightfully through the rest of our evening, and we retired to bed. I noticed that our entire house was "dead" quiet. I knew the ghosts were with us, but they were afraid and they were in hiding from the demon. I tried to sleep, but I didn't doze off until early morning. We both woke up at the same time because our extremely heavy waterbed was shaking and being lifted up and down. I screamed with fright, and I knew it was the demon. My husband thought it was an earthquake. I actually saw the end of our bed being picked up like it weighed nothing, and then it was dropped to our carpeted floor. I said out loud, "What the hell?" and then the demon held it up about one foot high and then waited a minute before it dropped us. The evil proceeded to do this too many times. I was so afraid and horrified of the demon. I yelled and told it to go back to hell from where it came from. At this time, I noticed large black finger bruises that had been inflicted on my leg during this chaos!

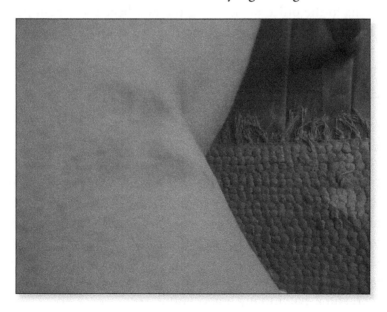

My husband, John, asked me what the hell had just happened. I told him he got the "hell" part right and that we were just introduced to our new house resident from hell. It wasn't leaving, and it was on a mission to kill me. This all sounds so weird but that is what the evil was planning to do!

My life has been very different compared to others. The following morning, I called a paranormal group located on the East Coast. I told them everything that had happened so far. They said they could help me. The group was very alarmed by my information. As I continued to speak to them, I became ill with horrible pain in my abdomen. I told them I needed to hang up, but they said it was the work of the demon to stop our conversation. The group informed me that "the demon reaches inside your body and pulls on your soul. You are actually under demonic attack, and this is only one way of many of how it will torment you!" This hurt so much that I always doubled over with pain.

The conversation with the paranormal group then ended for me when they needed two hundred up front for gas. They needed to add more money later for expenses. This would not work out for me. I was so disappointed because I felt this could be a scam. I did believe some of their information. I knew the demon stayed close to me, and it was always within striking distance.

Days had dragged by, and the demon had been very quiet. I just wanted it gone and to take all of its created problems for us with it. The normal ghosts in my house were not making noises for my attention. I was sure the demon was dominating them under this supernatural power. It was an unholy "quiet" throughout my house. I did not like it.

On this calendar date, Halloween was ten days away, and the paranormal action started picking up at our house. Our TVs, my washing machine, my dishwasher, etc. turned on and off by themselves.

One late afternoon, I was changing the sheets on a portable baby crib. I was looking down at the mattress when I heard a low-volume growl. It came from the corner of my son's bedroom. I continued to change the bed, and I did not react to the growl; and then I started to recite the Lord's Prayer. I knew it was the demon, and now

I had made it angry with me. I kept praying louder and louder! The demon kept growling louder, and its growl turned into a lion's roar. I wanted to cover my ears with my hands, but I didn't. The demon was trying to scare me, and it did. I did not look toward it because I didn't want to give it any satisfaction. I slowly turned and walked out of the room with my back toward it. I kept repeating the Lord's Prayer. I reached the staircase and decided to move a lot faster and grab my dog and my cell phone and then run to my backyard for safety. I called my husband and waited for his arrival. I hated the demon, and I knew it hated me; and it was not just at our home to scare us. It was here to end me.

It was three days before Halloween. I was running down the hallway of my house, and I somehow injured my meniscus in my left knee. I saw the doctor, and I went in the next day for emergency surgery. I was so worried about maybe missing Halloween. The doctor assured me that I would be walking normally for Halloween. It sounded like a good plan, but it didn't work that way. I was still unable to walk, and the big day was on time; but I wasn't. I was stuck in the recliner, and I was very crabby. I sat by myself in the early afternoon, and I angrily asked and yelled out loud for a real witch to visit me on All Hallows' Eve. I then added some stipulations to my request. No harm should happen to anyone, and the witch must leave by herself at the last stroke of midnight!

In preparation for Halloween, my husband and I had previously carved thirteen pumpkins before my surgery. He lit all the candles inside the pumpkins and placed them all near our front door. He also hung up homemade white-sheet ghosts I had sewn together. They all hung from the tree limbs, and it was so spooky how they all faced the same direction. I loved it!

Now it was Halloween evening, and dusk was settling in fast. John decided to take a picture of the glowing pumpkins. He used my cell phone camera. All of a sudden, he ran inside the house to my recliner; and he said there was something on our front door, and the flash just remained shining on the door! I peeled myself out of the recliner and used my crutches to reach the front door. I hobbled to the outdoors and turned around and saw what I didn't believe. She was on my front door! Yes! The witch had arrived. I didn't believe my own eyes. There was a manly yet womanly witch. She was a little ugly but not very scary. She was a modern-day witch. She was my witch! I was so excited that I almost jumped on my surgery leg. My husband also remarked that she was a witch. My witch request had arrived! I didn't tell John that I had wished for her just for my own Halloween surprise. My wish had come true! But really, how did this happen? I was a little afraid of her, and she looked very cunning and intimidating. We could only see her upper body down to her waist, yet her head was turned a little to her side; and her eyes were green and focused on me! (Yikes!) Her dark-orange hair was very short and looked like a man's haircut. As I previously mentioned, she resembled a man and a female with mixed features of both. Her eyes were slanted. She had a pointed nose and small ears that stuck outward. Her lips were of a woman, and her skin was a frog-green color. She had a quirky slight smile that made me wonder if she wanted to hurt me or was glad to see me. I also noticed everywhere I moved on the front lawn with my crutches, her eyes moved and followed me. This was so spooky, and I was so happy; yet I was cautious within her presence.

I stayed outside all evening so I could be close to the witch. I sat in a chair, and I passed out candy to trick-or-treaters. The parents walked with their trick-or-treaters, and they always asked my husband and me where we hid the projector to display such a realistic-looking witch. Sorry, no projector! The parents also asked us how we made the witch's eyes move as she watched their children and themselves, yet she always looked back to me. My husband and I told everyone it was a secret that we were trying out this Halloween. Everyone who saw the witch wanted to touch her. I couldn't let that happen because I didn't know how the witch would react. I wasn't sure of what she was capable of. The witch really stared at everyone, and she moved her eyes to examine all of them. Some people were frightened to see her eyes move, and they hurried and left to trick-or-treat elsewhere. Other people reacted just the opposite. They were in awe and commented on how gorgeous she was, and her eye movement made the entire decoration intriguing. Little did they know, she was an authentic witch. It was her idea to post herself on the front door in the unique way in which she did. It was perfect! This entire evening was awesome. The witch remained on the door, and she watched me as I snapped camera photos of my homemade ghosts. In my developed film, it revealed wisps of white mist near my hanging material ghosts and throughout my front yard. These were the real-deal ghosts enjoying Halloween night with me. I also took pictures of my four-foot-tall gargoyle statue that later revealed the coward demon was still with me and watching my every move. I captured its large yellow eyes on film staring at me as I was laughing with one of my friends. This particular photo was captured as the demon was inside the garage and looking outside through the window at me. Its head was tilted to one side in wonderment of what I was doing. It reminds me of my bulldog tilting his head when I talk to him. This is a sick picture of the demon watching me!

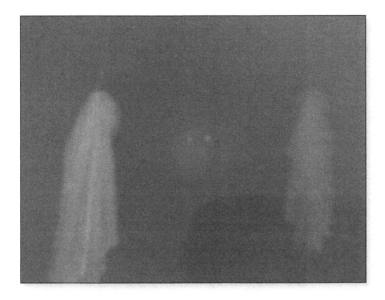

It was midnight, and I watched the witch slowly fade away. I waved to her and said thank you, and she sort of smiled at me. She was carrying out my original wish of peacefully leaving by herself by the last stroke of midnight. All Hallows' Eve had ended. I enjoyed the best Halloween I had ever had! The visitation from the witch, the real ghosts and, of course, the demon all combined actually scared me; and I didn't take any of these paranormal creatures lightly. This is a memory I will never forget! Now my question is, who should I ask to visit me this year for Halloween?

Thanksgiving was our next holiday, which was no fun at all. We were still under demonic attack. Sometimes, it growled at me in the car, but no one else could hear it. When we usually went grocery shopping, we always put our dog in his crate. I thought he would be safer there, but I was wrong. One day, we returned home after shopping, and our bulldog had been attacked in his dog crate. The poor thing had been stuck inside with the demon, and he couldn't fight for himself in such a small space. The demon scratched one side of Godzilla's face, gouging three deep, bloody scratches on his jowl. I cleaned him up; and he stuck to us like glue, and he wouldn't leave our side. I felt so bad for Godzilla. He was loved by us just like one of our children. After this incident, we never used the dog crate again. I caught on camera the disgusting invisible demon in front of an infant in a high chair as I took the baby's picture.

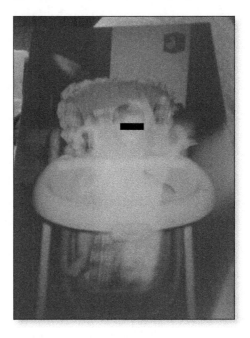

Thanksgiving turned out to be uneventful for our family; but Christmas was approaching, and I had a bad feeling about it. I chose to entertain our family on Christmas Eve. Our children and the grandchildren filled our house with fun and excitement. One disappointing phone call from my daughter of her cancellation for the evening was a large disappointment. My son-in-law and grandson still arrived, and we thoroughly enjoyed them. This was very concerning to me that my daughter was not with us, and I figured the demon was behind all of it. She really didn't have a specific reason for canceling.

Dinner and all the festivities ended around 10:00 p.m. I felt I was being watched all evening by evil as it followed me constantly throughout the house. Even though the suppression of its presence to me was evident our evening went well. I actually stayed awake past 3:00 a.m. picking up wrapping paper and washing dishes.

I prayed to God to make the demon leave us alone and leave our home.

I was finally tired enough to sleep; so I climbed up the thirteen steps to the upstairs, and I planned to watch television until my eyes were closed. My husband and Godzilla had retired to bed hours ago, and all I heard was snoring.

All of a sudden, my appetite went out of control. I was completely awake, and I craved the taste of baked ham. I wondered if the demon was scheming a surprise attack on me. I ignored that thought.

I crept out of the bedroom so I wouldn't wake my husband. I stopped at the top of the staircase. I stood there and listened, and there were no sounds anywhere. I felt as though I was in a huge suction cup, and the air surrounding me was muffled and way too quiet. I felt very uneasy, and I should have trusted my instincts. But I didn't, and I stepped down three steps. I stopped because I had the worst pain ever in my abdomen. It made me grab my lower stomach area, and it forced me to sit down. I knew it was the demon. I had fallen for his trick. I hated "it" so much.

I held on to the railing and the spindles on the staircase. He was going to kill me! I heard my voice only in my head and not in my ears. The voice said, "Ricky, go ahead and step down. You are at the bottom step." I answered with my thoughts, and I said, "The hell I am!" Now I knew it was ready to kill me! I then decided to send the demon my own mental telepathy back to it, and I told it to "go back to hell from where it came from, you son of a b——! In the name of our Father, the Son, and the Holy Ghost, who art in heaven!" I then continued sending the demon more telepathy of awful swear words I put together! Evidently, it received all my mental messages because it started taking away my human resources. I tried to loudly yell out help to my husband, and my voice was gone. I was still grasping the staircase for security as the demon made my body release all that I was hanging onto. I lost all control of myself as I watched my arms fall loosely to my sides.

I found a little air left inside of me, so I used it to ask God to help me. I succeeded, but I felt bad because I felt I was rude and I didn't say *please* to God at the end of my plea. Now I watched as my body was slowly standing up on the third step. I kept trying to take control of myself with a response from my own will. I tried to use my voice again, but no sounds came out of me. I had lost all control, and I had no feeling of contact with anything. With no voice and with my other senses failing, I wasn't even sure if I was breathing. Then my sight was taken, my hearing was gone, and my sense of smell was gone. I was totally disconnected from my body. I remember feeling so alone. I saw in my mind a blank white screen, yet I wasn't using my eyes to see it. This was a godsend to see the screen that had no flaws or specks or ripples of texture that I could find. Only black darkness would have frightened me a lot more than the white.

I knew God was with me, and I spoke to him with my own mind. I never had a panic attack, but I came close to it. At this point, I had no concept of time, and I felt I had lost my valuable human life. I couldn't even cry, but I still had thoughts and emotions in my mind. I actually felt sorry for myself. I wasn't sure if this demon situation would ever end.

I wondered if coma patients saw in their minds a white blankness as I did and not a frightening black. When we normally shut our eyes, we see darkness, but I think God gave us a white vision in our minds to make us feel safer.

I knew the demon had entered inside of me and had taken control of my body. In my mind, I kept asking God to help me, and I repeated this plea over and over again. The demon was still in control, yet I felt my leg and my footstep off of the third step down from the top of the stairs. OMG, the demon wanted me to feel my fright of falling and my soon-to-be death as I hit the wall and then the floor. The feeling of falling out of control and my speed traveling downward to my death was overwhelming. I knew he planned to take my soul and then proceed with breaking my neck and crushing my spine. The demon planned to falsely stage my body to have a fatal accident.

The demon's plan did not work! Near the end of my fall, I could actually see with my eyes a huge flash of light; and at the same instance, something gently caught me in midair. This happened before I hit the wall. I couldn't see very well because the light was so intense, yet it didn't hurt my eyes. I was so happy to be able to see again! My large toe on my right foot did hit the floor when I was caught by what I called an "angel." I was glad to be in touch with my body again even though my sensation was a pain in my toe. I welcomed it. I was gently held in midair with the bright light shining everywhere around me. Next, my body was gently turned around and lowered down on the rug. I felt as though I was floating. My fingertips slowly touched down first, and then my body was released. I felt warm and safe as the angel guarded above me.

Now I felt there was a standoff forming. The angel was my defender, and the demon still wanted me dead and the possession of my soul. Why me? My dark hallway had an invisible demon hiding in the corner and waiting for its chance to get me. I felt God's love and the devil's hatred at the same. This standoff was for possession of my soul. I was also thankful that God had sent help for me. I could feel this battle was ready to explode. Within the dead silence surrounding all of us, I couldn't take the stress of this battle anymore. I screamed and screamed for my husband. He and my bulldog ran down the stairs to help me. I could still feel the demon in the darkness as it began to slowly and cowardly slither back into the night.

The beautiful bright light had never left me. The demon knew I was protected from it. I felt as though the light caressed me one last time, and I felt loved and safe. I knew the demon was close, but I also knew that God was guarding me.

My husband did not see the bright light or even the darker-than-dark evil. I tried to tell him what had just happened, but I knew he didn't believe me.

I prayed that the demon had left my life, but I knew better.

After the demon attack, and it was the following morning, I found my cross necklace on top of the hallway rug. The sun's rays were shining and reflecting light from blue gems on it. The funny thing was the cross was still attached to the chain, and the clasp was still closed. My chain was too short to slip it over my head. This made me shiver. How did the demon remove it?

The following evening, I had a nail appointment scheduled with my best client and friend. She knew all about the demon from me. We were in my nail room, and I was somewhat gloating about how I had been saved and the demon had to leave my house. All of a sudden, we both heard a man's deep and loud voice start to laugh at me, and it gradually became louder and louder. It was in the open doorway to the nail room and was mocking me. The laughter soon changed to growls. I yelled at it to go back to hell to where it came from. After I talked back to it, the growls turned into a lion's roar. My best friend then told me she was afraid. That did it. I had to do something, so I jumped up from my chair and ran through the doorway and to the demon. The roaring abruptly stopped, and I evidently took it by surprise. There were no more sounds from the demon that day.

I finished the nail appointment, and we talked a lot. She told me she was going to talk to her preacher for advice. She was afraid for me.

Now I knew for sure that the demon was still close to me. It also took a couple of months before my resident ghosts had slowly come out of hiding and back to their own pranks again.

Finally, our lives were back to "our normal." Is the demon gone?

The End…or Is It?

ABOUT THE AUTHOR

There's no stopping Ricky Shick, author of *I'm Never Alone*! Since age five, paranormal and supernatural entities have communicated with her. She has prevailed through many life-threatening attempts. Ricky hopes that her personal knowledge and experiences will help others. She resides in Estes Park, Colorado, with her husband, John, and their bulldog Chopper. They share their town with one of America's most haunted hotels.

CPSIA information can be obtained
at www.ICGtesting.com
Printed in the USA
BVHW081222111121
621212BV00010B/1124

9 781662 433252